The
"Freshman ~~15~~ 16"
of Grief

The
"Freshman ~~15~~ 16"
of Grief

Losing My Forever Love & Finding My Way

Debbie Pausig

2024

www.Debbiepausigmft.com

First Printing: 2024

The Freshman ~~15~~ 16 of Grief/Debbie Pausig
ISBN:979-8-9912212-0-7

Book Layout © 2017 BookDesignTemplates.com

This book was printed in the United States of America.

THE TITLE

"The Freshman ~~15~~-16" of Grief"

It is not an error; it is a continuation. I started writing this book during the 15th year of grieving the death of my husband and my forever love. I am finishing it after completing my 16th year of grief. That extra year seemed pivotal in my grieving process, so I felt compelled to add it. Freshman "15" after all is a bit of a cliché, however there was more growth to share in year 16. My intention is for these cumulative years to create hope and the vision to keep moving forward for anyone who is grieving the death of a loved one. Your loved one is still walking beside you, just in a different plane of existence. My love is part of that spiritual existence.

Losing My Forever Love & Finding My Way

When you know, you know. I was a mere 17 going on 18 years old when after a few short weeks in college of dating him, I fell head over heels in love. I knew in that brief time that I would spend the rest of my life with him. Little did I know that I would spend the rest of "his" life with him. We had September 1977 to February 2008. Then he was gone, having died with the still in-curable Huntington's Disease. There I was a 48-year-old widow and single parent of two mid-teens. We had all suffered with the progressive devastating effects Huntington's Disease had on our family. I had lost the 25-year career of my young to mid adult-hood to an injury just three years prior. Two major life losses, two teens and no road map of life to help me find my way. Finding my way was provided by God who directed me to my "North Star," my purpose in both my personal and professional lives. Both personally and professionally, I humbly remain a work in progress.

COVER STORY

This is an actual illustration of my very own aging hands cradling a porcelain heart that has been broken and mended by the Kintsugi repair method that I will explain at the end of this book.

My hands are wrapped by my familiar warm, fuzzy and mink like soft blanket. The blanket is representative of two things, my community of friends and family that have held me with love and support in the grief and growth I have experienced during these Freshman 15 16 years and beyond. It also represents the irregular ebb and flow of the grieving process. With each fold, swirl, curve, hairpin turn, peak and valley I have learned that grief is not a linear process. At times it is smooth as the soft faux mink texture. Other times it is hidden in between the dark cavernous creases. Be not fooled by the appearance of the beautiful color and inviting texture. For when grief resides in the creases, at any given time, it does rear its ugly head. And when it does, the cracked heart feels that pain once again as if it was the first time. That first time it was fractured.

My whole loving heart was once like a beautiful time piece. It ran like the finest watch made with Swiss movement. Just before and after the death of my forever love, my grieving heart's inner workings fractured and changed forever. Unlike the watch, a griever's heart cannot be repaired by a master watchmaker. The hearts cracks mend and produce scars that no one on the outside world can see. Grieving is hard and challenging work, each and every fracture line alters the griever's function. It is the most personal work one can do. There is no cure for grief as it is a lifelong process. What we can do is spend our lifetime mending ourselves by doing the best to find our way through this process. Perhaps those cracks create their own roadmap of possibilities in life we would have never been exposed to had it remained whole. Our assumptive world would have put us on the highway traveling through life as "we" expected it to be. Our losses create the "de-tours," those off the beaten path experiences we would have never chosen unless we were detoured. Loss is our detour. Is that the mystery of our true destiny? Navigating the detours? Following the other GPS: God's Positioning System to our personal North Star?

CONTENTS

Dedications

To my late husband Perry Pausig, the love of my life, my muse, the one who gave me, in life and in death, the drive to honor him by helping others the best way I can within my means. We travel on the paths of two different planes as he guides me to the adventures that are still yet to be held in this life.

To my children Kate and Daniel. We have all grieved in our own way over the last 16 years. You have watched my process of healing myself and others and supported my many paths of continuing to live while still holding the love of your dad within.

To my mentor, the late Sr. Mauryeen O'Brien, O.P. who died in 2023 in joyous reunion with the Lord. She cultivated and cheered me on as I chose this new life's purpose of working with grief, loss, and bereavement from the moment she trained me in 2008 to her deathbed.

To my friends, my angels, who have supported me in grief and in friendship and are brave and strong enough to answer my calls and texts, no matter the time or day. Thank you for holding my hand, providing a shoulder to cry on, for including me in your lives, and for tolerating my sick sense of humor. You are the ones who provide what I need to make it through the day mentally, emotionally and spiritually. I am thankful that you have taken the time to "pack my parachute" with the supports that have helped me through this grieving and aging process to date. You are the parachute packers who have silently contributed to my successes. And, I hope I have taken time to pack your parachute as well.

"Who's packing your parachute?" Charles Plumb was a US Navy jet pilot in Vietnam and POW now motivational speaker. https://www.youtube.com/watch?v=SCblO3SLPXI

Losing My Forever Love

Goodbye My Love, Perry

February 27, 2008, was a date that rained all night into the day. God was sharing our tears of sadness. Morning came and the nurses cleaned him up. As he lay motionless, breathing erratically, I stroked his full head of blonde and graying hair with my fingers.

Huntington's Disease (HD) had transformed the man I once knew. His once tall slender athletic built body was now tall and skinny with atrophied muscles. Muscles that once graced his arms, shoulders and neck had dissolved. All that remained were boney structures jutting from the cheeks in his face, collarbone, hips, knees, and ankles covered with pale tissue paper thin skin. No longer could I see the eyes that sparkled like Caribbean blue topaz. His smile was no longer able to express that coy mischievous and boyishness I once knew. The affectless mouth was a barely functioning opening allowing for inhaling and exhaling.

I gently caressed his face with my hands while I wept. I knew by his breathing that his time was nearing its end. I whispered softly to him that it was okay for him to go. We had a good life together. He was a good husband and Dad. I told him that I loved him so very much. As hard as it was, I knew it was the right thing for me to do. But he was not ready yet. He waited.......

He waited for his dad and older brother to arrive and joined me by his bedside. He needed to be near and hear his family just one last time. The night before, he was near and heard his sister. Now he was near and hearing his dad and brother; he was complete.

He was positioned on his left side facing me. He had to be on his side to prevent choking on his saliva and for drainage. I was able to stroke his hair with my right hand and his face with my left. Dad was to my right close to his entire head. His brother sat directly across from me. He was able to rub the back of his head and back.

We sat in silence. We wept in silence while we listened. We listened as his breathing became labored. We listened to the deafening silence between his few last breaths. I can only describe how focused I was on him, his face, and my sorrow as he continued to slip away from this earthly realm. We heard "one last breath" at 1:18 PM on February 27, 2008. The man we all loved, the man we sat vigil over was no longer. Dad put his arm around me and said, "It's over now." We hugged. I was so thankful to have them with me at this critical moment. I will never forget that neither of us (Perry nor I) was physically alone during his last hours and moments. We were not alone spiritually either; God had gently taken Perry home to be reunited with his mother.

It was now a critical period. Perry had decided to donate his brain to science. In order to preserve the brain, the nurses put a huge bag of ice under his head. The funeral home had been contacted to transport Perry to a local hospital morgue as soon as possible to remove the brain for transport to Mass General where it would be studied as his mother's was.

A Spiritual Transition

As I kept vigil over Perry's dead body, I adorned it with our 25th Wedding Anniversary Hawaiian Lei I had brought to his hospital room. I then witnessed something I had only seen as special effects in a movie. I saw a golden shimmer rise from his chest area and dissipate upward into the air. I had a strong feeling that Perry's spirit had just left the vessel we call the human body.

When I looked back at his body, it resembled any other dead body I had ever seen. There was a "dead body look" I have seen as pale skin, eyes partially open and mouth partially open from his last breath. It is a "look I've seen before where the ill has died."

I use this description because I have seen dead bodies during my career in police work.

My heart and soul were convinced that Perry's essence, his spirit left his body at that time. It had been trapped in that sickly human vessel for too long. For the first time in "many" years, his spirit was FREE!! Free to be! Free to Soar! Free of HD!!!

After his body was picked up by the funeral home, I walked to my car and cried. As I cried, I noticed that it had stopped raining. I gazed at the western sky through my tear swollen eyes and saw the beginnings of a beautiful sunset. God was reassuring me that Perry's spirit was free.

A Special Place in The Sky Called Heaven

As I lay in bed the evening of Perry's death, I stared out my bedroom window. In the clear dark sapphire evening sky, I saw the biggest and brightest twinkling star in the southeast. He was giving me a sign that he made it to Heaven. Now, he was okay.

I talk to that star quite often. It has moved but is still very present for me. For the heck of it, I Googled, "What is the bright star in the southeastern sky?" Google's response was the planet "Jupiter." Though his body is no longer in my presence, Perry's spirit continues to soar. I feel it and sometimes see it. And it gives me great comfort.

Perhaps they are not stars,

But rather openings in heaven

Where the love of our lost ones

Pours through and shines down upon us.

To let us know they are happy."

Eskimo Proverb quote

Me a WIDOW!!!

15 16 years ago

Who would have imagined that ~~15~~16 years ago I would be widowed? We were young, only 48 and 50 years old. The disease we suffered with, Huntington's Disease (HD), took shape and took our middle and old age away from us. Our hopes, our dreams, the thought of retiring together shattered and now a distant memory.

My heart, like that exquisitely crafted Swiss Watch that once beat with precise movement broke when I knew it was time for hospice care. For 34 days, I watched the shadow of death creep toward his body that lay in that hospital bed. During his last moments on this earth his eyes fixed and stared toward the plane, not on this earth and the last breaths growing longer in duration and then the final exhale. It was 1:18pm on February 27, 2008, ~~fifteen~~ sixteen years ago. Little did I know then I was about to enter what I am coining "The Freshman ~~15~~ 16 (years) of Grief". You will see the Freshman 15 has changed to the Freshman 16. It is because I started writing this book in earnest during the 15th year. I am finishing it after completing my 16th year of grief. That extra year seemed pivotal in my grieving process, so I felt compelled to add it. Freshman 15, after all, is a bit of a cliché; however, there was more growth to share in year 16. My intention is for these cumulative years to create hope and the vision to keep moving forward for anyone who is grieving the death of a loved one. Your loved one is still walking beside you, just in a different plane of existence. My love is part of that spiritual existence.

Not about early grief

Many books have been written about early grief. It is not surprising because it is sharp and raw like a newly broken piece of glass. It cuts deep, hurts deep, and sometimes it is as if we cannot stop the bleeding. This book is different. This one has a time lapse of 16 years. There are times when shards of glass manage to find me and re-open my early wounds of grief. It hurts like hell, and I am still bleeding! Now not as often and for shorter amounts of time. And at other times, the edges of the glass are smooth like sea glass having tumbled in the ocean. The wound is covered by a scar of resilience unaffected by the smooth glass as I too am tumbling in the ocean of life. This is as much a book on grieving the death of a beloved spouse as it is grieving during the aging process without that beloved.

"The Freshman ~~15~~ 16"

We usually refer to the "Freshman 15" as the expected pounds a college freshman may gain. Have I gained 16 pounds in my 16 years of grief? Thankfully, no. Because grief is a lifelong process, l am referring to the "Freshman 16" as my first 16 years in grief since my beloved died in 2008, it is now 2024! It's been 10 years since I published my first book, *"An Affaiя Worth Remembering With Huntington's Disease"* and I have just completed the 10th

Anniversary Edition of that book. There is something about the aging process without my beloved over the last 16 years that has created this poignant reminder that we did not have the privilege of growing old together. When he died: I did not have the wrinkles I have today; I did not have the natural "tinsel" that frames my face; I was not wearing progressive lenses (I do not think); and I was not old enough for an AARP card. Fast forward, wrinkles-√, silver streaks-√, AARP card (and its perks!)-√, Progressive lenses getting stronger every year-√, and the age of Medicare is knocking loudly at my door and is HERE to stay! I think what started me on the thoughts of writing this book was the year **he** would have turned "65" in 2002. And now it is my turn!

"Angelversary"

As each death anniversary or "Angelversary" rolls around, I get the feeling in my being as if the loss is new all over again. An "Angelversary" is the date people remember their loved one died. February 27, 2024, was the 16th Angelversary. It was also the 16th entry into my annual grief journal that I only write in on the Angelversary. It was also the first time I looked back and read the very first entry on February 27, 2009.

For those of you who feel the similar experience, isn't it like watching the 1993 film "Ground Hog Day"?

In contrast to the movie, I DO NOT re-live my husband's death over and over. What is repeated as the day approaches are the feelings of sadness and emptiness in my heart. The cracks now formed by scar tissue that forever remains. The heart, which was once whole is forever broken and scarred, so permanent as the love I lost. Though mending, I still feel that scar within, not visible to the outside world. Only to my inner self. It is quite unlike all the surgical scars I bear on the outside that are easily seen. Those lines of the cracks that bonded the broken pieces seem to surface as the day approaches. My mind gets distracted, but the heart remembers. I have a heart shaped pendant that has a stained-glass pattern. It bears only two colors, black and white. As I look at it, I am reminded of the black portions in my heart that died with him. I am also reminded of the white portions that represent the life I am still living. That pendant is a symbol that death and life co-exist in me and in so many others that are still breathing and can feel their own pulse every day after the death of a loved one. This co-existence will last my lifetime.

The Three Jars

A tangible illustration of grief that I have used in my therapy practice, support groups and presentations is Dr. Lois Tonkins theory from 1996 where people seem to think that grief shrinks with time. What actually happens is that grief remains the same, it is our world around the grief that changes, if we let it. Picture three different size mason jars, small, medium, and large. I put the exact same size squishy ball inside the jars. That squishy ball represents our grief. My current squishy "ball" is a red heart because that is where the grief resides, in my heart. In the beginning grief encompasses our entire being as if it is squeezed in the smallest jar. The grief remains the same size in the medium jar, what changes is the space around it. And in the large jar, grief remains the same, yet there is even more space. That growing space in the medium and large jars is LIFE, if you welcome it into your existence. I currently reside in the large jar as my life and world have grown around my grief. However, on occasions such as birthdays, wedding anniversaries and death anniversaries, my world reduces to the small jar in memory of my loved one, temporarily acknowledging my loss. I then resume living in either the big or medium jar once again. It is a dynamic and fluid process. If it were static that would indicate a problem of being stuck and clinically significant for the length of sixteen years.

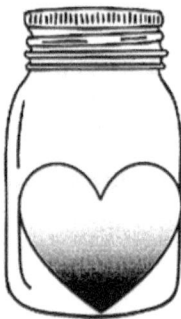

Friendly warning

Be forewarned, this book includes some warped humor as it is a coping skill I have mastered in my lifetime. It is my failsafe from my adverse childhood experiences, 25 years in police work, experiencing loved one's deaths, other losses both death and non-death related and my current work in death and dying and bereavement.

This book is about my time of being lost and found over my "Freshman 16" and the curiosity of what is next. Might there be sequels: The Sophomore? The Junior? The Senior? Who knows? Perhaps if I relocate to a Blue Zone and live longer to tell more.

A line from "Seasons of Love" from the movie made from the Broadway show "Rent" has recently circled in my mind…."Five hundred, twenty-five thousand, six hundred minutes…." So, I let Google do the work and it calculated: "Eight million, four hundred fifteen thousand three hundred and sixty minutes." That is 192 Months; 834.857 Weeks; 5,844 Days; 140,256 Hours; 8,415,360 Minutes; and 504,921,600 Seconds! But who is counting! Not me until I had the brainstorm of looking it up. That is my 16 years of seasons of love. That is a long time without him and God willing, I will have that and many more to go in this life because I am not done yet.

Notes:

The 16-year span of this book is divided into four parts. Each part illustrates a four-year journey of death anniversary or Angelversary journal entries. Each chapter will begin with my actual journal entry in italics at the exact time it was written. The words and the punctuation may not make sense to you and that is okay. How I wrote it was where my thoughts and emotions were on each one of those days. I put my annual thoughts of sorrow and hope into words. If you have ever grieved deeply, you will understand. I have deliberately excluded pieces of my journal pertaining to my personal thoughts related to my children. This was done to respect their own personal grief journeys.

I included the entries I posted on social media Facebook beginning in 2010 to the last entry for this book in 2024. As I grew as a person and grief therapist, I thought it appropriate for the "professional" to be seen and "heard" as an actual griever. One entry response was highlighted as it captured what I was trying to share with those in my social media world.

I included a number of poems written when my emotions were raw. They too may not be grammatically correct or make sense. To me, the griever, it was a way of therapeutically expressing those raw emotions. It is the imperfections in the raw work that may only make sense to me, the griever. Those I will not change. They were the reality of the moment in my grief. True and unadulterated, they remain unchanged.

Each journal entry concludes with a reflection of what I re-member as of this writing in 2024. The reflections give insight and perspective thanks to the education, life, work, and growth I have experienced since that entry and who I am today as I con-tinue to find my way.

You will find that the references of "He, Him, You, and Your" are used interchangeably for Perry. There was only one Perry in my life for without him there would not be the first book nor the continuation of my story in this one.

Since this is not a textbook, I will cite resources within the body of my reflections.

I have taken the opportunity to include some of my own pro-fessional works in the Appendix Section of this book.

The Freshman Poems: Grief is My Muse

It is an interesting process, writing poems and writing in general. When I am emotional, I do my best work. I think about the Platinum Album of a singer. The good stuff is full of emotion. Life, Death, Break-ups, Love, Hate, etc. provide the depth of emotion that screams to be told via song. Once it is released it is universally relatable on so many levels. We grab it, digest it, hold it, and release what does not serve us.

Many of the poems were created within the first two years following the death of my husband. Others were created a few years later. Some were even revised. They are part of the evolution of my grieving process. In death, he remains the age he was, a young 50 years old. Actually, in my heart, I prefer to remember him as a vibrant 35-year-old before the indescribable wrath Huntington's Disease took on his body, mind, and spirit. In life, I have changed. Had I not, I would be horribly stuck in the past as if living my life in the rear-view mirror instead of looking through the windshield of a car at what is ahead of me, this thing called Life.

I hope you enjoy reading these poems that were written when grief held a visceral place in my very being. They may or may not make sense to you and that is okay. They did to me at the time they were written. There is no right or wrong way to grieve. Writing poems created a catharsis in helping me put my grief into words. My dearly departed had the gift of prose in our relationship from the very beginning 47 years ago. These poems are another way I honor him.

Sea Glass-1

Grief hurts, its pain is real and sharp.
Like a glass bottle thrown into the sea,
we start out whole.

The loss of a loved one breaks us,
like the bottle that is smashed against the rocks.
It breaks into pieces with sharp, jagged edges.

Only with time,
the sharp glass tumbles in the ocean
and its edges smooth.

As with grief,
only with time
the sharp hurt will go away.
09-08-08

Christmas Sea Glass

I've never done something like this before,
To spend Christmas Day searching the shore.

Something special brought me here,
A remembrance of the day near 10 months before.
A trip to CT Hospice to thank the Angels who cared,
For my love till the last breath, he did sigh.
To not go I would have called myself scared,
To not thank them would cause my inner self to cry.

I went, I thanked, I left.
So glad I did then to visit his brick.
With a scarf I framed it and took a quick pic
I must be here because of St. Nick!
Along the path of so many beloved
A feeling of peace had come over me.
Was it my actions or was it the sea?

A short drive away was old Branford Point
A view of CT Hospice from there I could see,
The exact view from my Love's window
where he would last be.
It's Christmas Day 2008 and the Point I would comb,
For beach glass once sharp and broken like our home.

But it's Christmas Day when the Lord was born,
And now the beach glass is tumbled and worn.
My Love is with the Lord and the warm sun shines.
Glistening on the water like a sparkling pathway,
His sign from heaven, "It's A New Day"
"I'm good here he says and I'm finally free,
I'm at peace and so shall you be.

A new year is coming, there are things you must do,
Go out and LIVE with our children!

I did not leave you alone.
I promised you this.
Don't give up on life.
It's LIFE you must not miss.

For I am watching from high above.
And I'll never forget it was me you did love.

A cup of Sea Glass you collected on this Christmas Day
A cup of hope and healing I sent your way."
12-26-08

I Bought Myself a Heart Today

I bought myself a heart today
It reminds me of my own.
Two shades in its visual display
One near, one far from home.
Somewhat fractured like the real thing
Yet bound together naturally.
Parts are white and parts are black
One looks forward, the other back.
White is the present and future ahead.
Black is what's missing, the part that's dead.
My Love is gone
And forever he'll be
In my mind and in my heart
From now until eternity.
02-16-09

A Sapphire Ring

A sapphire ring I bought for you
A reminder of my love so true
So dark a blue as the deep blue sea
So deep the love between you & me
Oval in shape as the track we once ran
Back to a time I discovered you were my man
Held by four prongs it is set
As you in my heart with no regrets
Encircled by a white gold rope
I stare and sigh and try to cope
A small trail of diamonds can then be seen
To finish the piece so beautiful and serene
Our daughter said it's the color of the sea
The deep blue love between you and me.

02-19-09

Castaway Cay

It happened before
But I'll never know
From where I've been
Or where I'll go
This poem is being written
From where I will be
For a short time longer
At Castaway Cay
The cruise is now ending
It's one thing for sure
Like a branch I'll be bending
Enduring life's chore.
02-20-09

The Waves Come Rushing

The waves come rushing
Some strong and some frail
I walk the sand combing
And searching to no avail
Before I step forward the waves crash on in
Covering where I'm going
And where I had been
I search for some shells
And there's coral too
Shredded seaweed aplenty
And a starfish to boot.
A photo of all I will take with me
And return Gods treasures back to the sea.

02-20-09

28 February 2009

It happened again like the year before.
Gone on the 27th, on the 28th evermore.
One difference this time I don't know why
last year you shown as a bright star in the sky.
You signaled from heaven
twinkling bright I could see.
From my bedroom window your soul set free.
A year makes a difference for last night
it did rain.
Perhaps a sign of cleansing for without pain
there is no gain.
One big similarity I can honestly say,
was the bright sun in the morning the very next day.
A sign from the night sadness.
It's A New Day!
I told our son that his dad was in heaven
The perfect fishing hole for him
the good Lord did find.
A place of beauty for one gentle and kind.

Don't fret my son,
I'll be with you forever.
02-28-09

The Beach

I walk along the beach
watching the waves tell the story of my life
as it was and what is to be.

I walk on the sand leaving impressions.
I look back at my past
quickly disappearing
from sight
but not my memory or heart.

I look ahead to sand that is new,
Awaiting my steps to create a memory,
An impression of the present,
And future which is a vast canvas yet to impress.
02-02-09

Back to the Beach

Back to the beach and ocean I find myself.
I walk along the sand and see the footprints
of where I was.

A wave comes in and erases what was
An interesting process it is
I move on in my journey
having left a mark
that quickly disappears with time.

My grief too will disappear in time
My footprints, the places where I've been
are recycled with the waves
creating a new canvas for me to travel onward
not backward retracing what was.

Forward I go and grow from what was.
To look back into the past I see nothing remains.
What does remain are the memories imprinted
In my heart and soul
Never to be washed away
Always to be in me.
02-09-09

Sea Glass-2

*Like a fresh piece of glass entering the sea for the first
time, our wounds of loss are also sharp.*

*Like the weathered sea glass,
in time we too will be smooth and be able to
tumble with life's changing tides.*

*The painful wound left by our loss
will slowly heal.
As the healing begins, a scar forms,
now a permanent reminder of our loss.*

*In time the scar may gently fade but its presence
will never be forgotten.*

*We wear the scar like a badge of honor
for our lost love.
It is with honor we remember our time
with our loved one.*

*Our loved one will never be forgotten,
like the scar,
they are present within us eternally.*

*It is not until the healing that they can become
emotionally relocated in us
and we can move onward.*
09-08-13

Sea Glass-1 revised

The pain of grief is sharp and surreal.
Like a glass bottle thrown into the sea,
we start out whole.

The loss of a loved one breaks us,
like the bottle smashed against the rocks.

We break into sharp jagged pieces.
In time, the sharp glass tumbles in the ocean
and its edges smooth.

With grief,
our emotions feel tumbled and tossed.
In time,
the sharpness lessens.
09-23-13

Sea Glass-2 revised

*Like a fresh piece of glass entering the sea for the first
time, my wounds of loss are also sharp.*

*Like the glass, in time I too will be smooth from tumbling
with life's changing tides.*

*The painful wound left by my loss will slowly heal.
As I heal, a scar forms,
it is now a permanent reminder of my loss.*

*In time the scar may gently fade but its presence
will never be forgotten.*

*My scar is worn like a badge of honor
for my lost love.
With love I remember and honor
my time with my loved one.*

*My loved one will never be forgotten, like the scar,
it is present within me eternally.*

*With healing my loved one has settled into
a special place within me.*

Once again, I can move.

09-23-13

Sea Glass-3

Like the ocean waves,
grief may come and go.

Once sharp discarded glass has adjusted
to its new environment, the sea.

It might be collected by a beachcomber and start a new
journey out of the ocean.

Or it could continue tumbling in its current
environment one day at a time
taking on changes through adjustment and
acceptance with new beginnings.

09-08-13

Sea Glass-3 revised

Grief, like ocean waves, may come and go.
Once sharp discarded glass adjusts to
its new environment, the sea.

I too am adjusting to this new environment until a wave
strikes with a vivid reminder of my loss.

The glass might be collected by a beachcomber and start
a new journey out of the ocean.

Or it could continue tumbling in the sea,
one day at a time,
facing the unknown.

I am a piece of sea glass.
Sometimes I'm stable as if wedged between rocks.
Sometimes I am tumbling with the tides.

And sometimes I am thrust by a tsunami like force
against the sand,
displaced from one environment to another.

I am changed from my loss.
09-23-13

Sea Glass-1 revision #2

The pain of grief is sharp and surreal
Like a glass bottle thrown into the sea,
we start out whole.

The loss of a loved one breaks us.
Like the bottle smashed against the rocks,
we break into sharp jagged pieces.

Our heart and very being is cut with every thought
of our loved one no longer with us.
In time, the sharp glass tumbles in the ocean
and its edges smooth.

With grief, our emotions feel tumbled and tossed.
In time, the sharpness lessens.
The tumbling continues in a gentler motion.

The storms of their death anniversary,
their birthday, our special occasions are a reminder
that our love is forever.
It is a blessing to feel the storms of pain.
They remind us of the love of grief.
If we did not love so deeply,
we would not grieve.

01-21-18

Part One
Years One to Four

2008-2009

Journal Entry

02-26-09: A year ago today they called to say, your body was failing come right away.

It was Daniel's Birthday and I reminded you so, to last through this day I ordered you not to go.

You held on to be aware of one last evening, a gathering of family and friends it did bring.

With stories and laughter, we surrounded you well, so pleased we were there surely I could tell.

I held you and caressed you with all of my love.

My hands felt your body preparing for heaven above.

Losing you made my heart torn and tattered,

hanging on through Dan's Birthday is all that mattered.

02-27-09: It was one year ago this very day,

we said goodbye in our own special way.

In my hands you were till the last breath you breathe,

I reminded you just how much you did achieve.

Our hopes and our dreams each one truly met,

our love and our children you'll never forget.

1:18 pm was your final breath,

known to me as the time of your death.

A transformation of your spirit shortly after I did see,
from your body the earthly vessel you were set free.
Enroute to heaven your soul ascended above,
The Lord awaited you arms open with LOVE...
my heart dark with sadness my eyes with tears bawling.
I watched you "crossover" a year ago today,
I insisted you leave Hospice in a very special way.
On to eternal life donning a Hawaiian lei,
I released your body to the morticians with few words to say.
Your head rested on ice during this physical transfer,
Preserving your brain for science, your donation for a cure.
It was your dying wish to help cure this disease.
To end the suffering of so many pleas.
Your body was released from Hospice today,
Ending a 34 day journey your last silent say.
As I exited the building, I saw the rain had ceased,
The sky clearing, from the clouds, the sun released.
Was it the Lord's sign Perry's suffering was through?
It must have been because the grey sky was turning blue.
I walked to my car, got in and cried,
Life as I knew it now my first love, my soul mate,
My heart had just died.
****

At 1:14 pm today I prayed to you Lord and to Perry. Preparing myself for the exact time, 1:18 pm, a year ago you took your last breath. I sat on our back deck feeling the warmth of the sun through a clouded sky. As the moment of 1:18 pm struck, a strong wind began howling and continues to do so. I prayed to the Lord and to Perry thanking you for your guidance over the last year. I pray for guidance as I'm guessing these winds are signaling a change is coming. Perhaps weather related, I'd rather think Divine.

A new "sign" for me to go forth with my life and do what I am guided to do. I will now finish the devotional "Through a *season of grief" completing its 365 days of support in what was my most difficult year of bereavement.*

Through Perry's illness I found God. Through Perry's death, I became closer to the Lord in my daily living. I pray regularly and have faith in what is in store for me. My faith is strong and will continue to be. I believe God will give me the strength to accomplish what I seek to do. With patience and continued hard work and perseverance, I can accomplish great things while I am on this earth by helping others the best way I can, as Perry did during his shorter time with us.

Reflections.....

Wow, I reflected back on that day and nothing else that happened during that first year. Much more did happen indeed! This was a whole new chapter of grief. After death grief for me and for our two teenage children. We grieved the losses Huntington's Disease took from us for so many years, now it was the actual loss of life and presence of my husband, their father.

The Year of Firsts

It was a year of firsts. Our lives had changed so much from the illness that we were not used to celebrating like when you were well. Looking back, the Christmas season was the only thing that stood out. Christmas Eve was with moms' side of the family here. Christmas Day was different. I did not go to your dad's. I felt like a man without an island. Mom the kids and I ended up eating at a Chinese restaurant and then dropped off a basket of cookies to hospice, the place you died. We just drove around and wandered

The Common and Normal Feelings

According to J. William Worden in his book Grief Counseling and Grief Therapy, the feelings I felt were normal in the grieving process. I felt **sad** over the loss of my loved one. I felt **anger** for now being alone and a single parent. **Guilt** is a common feeling. I had no guilt or regrets. **Anxiety** in wondering how I was going to deal with my own grief and the children's. I ended up focusing on their grief and surviving as head of the household putting my grief on what I thought was "on hold." Only to learn later that I allowed myself to grieve a little at a time, dosing it. **Loneliness** is feeling the permanence of the loss. Perry was no longer in his chair or bedroom. **Fatigue** is common. Grieving is exhausting physically and emotionally. **Shock** can occur when a lengthy illness ends abruptly in death even though it had been expected any time. Sometimes people just keep bouncing back. It is most common in sudden and unexpected deaths. **Yearning** for the person who died is common. **Relief** that a long, suffering, or painful illness is finally over. We hate seeing our loved ones suffer. **Numbness** is nature's way of protecting us from the overwhelming onslaught of painful feelings all at one time.

Secondary Losses

There were other losses that happened after the death. Some were immediate, others took time to realize. They become that ripple in the pond created by the pebble of death. Here are a few examples of secondary losses I experienced. **Loss of identity,** I lost a large part of myself. I was no longer a spouse, partner, companion, best friend, caregiver and part of the Perry and Debbie couple we were for 31 years. **Loss of family structure** our family structure had become unbalanced from Huntington's Disease. It regained balance after the death however the structure was no longer the foursome of mother, father, child, child. It was now a single parent with two children. Most profoundly was **the loss of my past.** My witness to life from age 17 to 48 was gone. The person I reminisced with and made memories with was gone. **Loss of future,** though our dreams of growing old together and retiring were destroyed with the disease. I had no dreams and no one to dream with as we approached our golden years. **Loss of trust,** how could I risk getting into another relationship? What if my partner got sick? Could I love that deeply again to caregive the way I did my husband? **Loss of sharing** those daily goings on. Other secondary losses include **loss of control, loss of patience with self, loss of one's own health issues and others.** That death pebble can ripple far and wide if you sat down and made a list.

A New Day

Not long after Perry died, a funny thing happened to me one day when I was leaving church. It sounds like the preamble to an old Rodney Dangerfield joke except it is not. A wonderful nun, Sr. Jacinta, approached me and "suggested" I get trained to facilitate a bereavement group in church. I find it hard to say no to a nun. In my case, one that is as kind, loving and persuasive as this one. *I think they receive intense training in the art of persuasion.* I listened to her suggestion and a new door opened. Knowing of the recent death of my husband, she suggested I get trained in a bereavement program called "New Day." She had hoped I would facilitate a bereavement group at our church with her and another parishioner. I facilitated New Day groups for seven years.

How could I say no? Besides, what I have learned, and it remains our joke to this day, is I cannot say no to the nuns. They suggest, not ask. Before I knew it, I was trained along with Sr. Jacinta and another widow named Helen by Sr. Mauryeen O'Brien, O.P. who was the creator of the program and Coordinator of the Divorced, Separated and Bereaved programs at the Family Life Office, Archdiocese of Hartford. She trained us in her New Day support program for the bereaved. We were trained only a month and a half after Perry's death and commissioned as "Ministers of Consolation" in April 2008.

Our first facilitation of the New Day Program ran for 10 weeks from September to November 2008. It was my first experience working with the bereaved, other than myself. During this first program, I witnessed something incredible. I saw people enter the group and transform from being shrouded in darkness to allowing cracks of light to enter their darkness. This was visible with a smile, even laughter. I also received my own healing in bereavement from helping others in this program. This experience had begun the journey in finding my way to my North Star, my future purpose and calling; but not before the firsts had to be addressed.

2009-2010

Signs, Signs in 2009!

- *3/2009: Email from an old high school classmate her initials then were P.B., her married name is "Perry". Initials P.P.*
- *7/2009: San Jose, CA; The Gold Mustang with black convertible top- I rejected 2 rental cars because I could not see out the high back window. The rental agency finally presented Daniel and I with the Gold Mustang. Perry owned a 1968 Gold Mustang with a black vinyl top.*
- *7/2009: Pelican Point Lighthouse, Santa Cruz "P.P" Pelican Point Lighthouse book author, Frank Perry.*
- *7/2009: Car license plate frame: Perry Mitchell, LLC.*
- *7/2009: In SF, Huntington Park near the intersection of California St. Huntington Park, CA is where Perry was born.*

"Angelversary" Social Media Posts on Facebook Start

February 27, 2010
Two years ago today I held life and death in my hands. I witnessed his spirit leave his body for its journey to Heaven. Forever in my heart, eternally with the Lord. Perry Pausig 04/06/57-02/27/08.

Reflections......

I cannot find it; the journal entry is not there! Where did it go?

I know I took the kids away for Daniel's 16th Birthday 2009 in the effort to soften the blow of this second anniversary. Of course, I know now that it probably did not matter. My grief journaling in February 2009 is reflected in poems section that I wrote during our trip.

Another "Calling"

Amazing things occur with a little help from God above "if" you are open and allow them to. It was an honor to be chosen to facilitate the New Day Program and be in the humble presence of the bereaved. This opened my spirit to another "calling" and another sign from Perry.

Then "it" happened. It was a calling as strong as the ones I received to pursue a career as a police officer when I was 17 and again when it was time for parenthood when I was 33. This calling was a future in working with the bereaved. It was a sign for me to go forth with my life to serve where I am guided to by my "GPS", my North Star. I was to fulfill that future in working with the bereaved. First, this required a reinvention of self. Funny that "reinvention" sometimes occurs around the time we get that introduction to AARP card in the mail at the age of 50. Although, that reinvention required that I go back to college and further my education with another master's degree. I already had my bachelor's and one master's degree. They were connected with my old life, my police life, and not this new one.

I decided to formalize this new path with an appropriate master's degree. The question is which one? I looked into three different master's degree offerings, Social Work, Counseling and Marriage and Family Therapy. After researching the three, the one that stood out for me was the Master's in Marriage and Family Therapy (MFT) Program right in my back yard at Southern Connecticut State University. I chose Southern's MFT program because it focused on working with the family system. What brought me to this point was that Huntington's Disease, the disease Perry died from, rocked our family system of four. It applied to us so much that I ended up using our example as a case study paper. I also wanted to work with Trauma and Grief. I wanted to add certifications that weaved together my police and personal life experiences. I wanted to treat individuals, couples and families experiencing depression, anxiety, caregiving, trauma, loss, grief, bereavement, long term, chronic progressive, terminal illnesses, and lifecycle changes. My road as a marriage and family therapist and grief counselor/therapist was the path to follow.

The mission was accomplished through intense hard work, dedication, the addition of 17 extra pounds, and bunch of new tinsel on my scalp (gray hairs). Looks like the Freshman ~~15~~, 16 was the Freshman "17" for a very brief period early on. I earned a Master of Family Therapy Degree (MFT) and subsequent certifications as a Certified Clinical Trauma Professional (CCTP) and

Certified in Thanatology: Death, Dying and Bereavement (CT). I am so proud of these personal/professional achievements and now the ability to go forth and work with those in need of my services.

Another Loss On the Horizon

As I rounded the year of 2009-2010, another piece of grief was on the horizon. We just celebrated mom's 80th birthday. A month later her oncologist suggested that she not make plans past July 2010. Mom was experiencing some significant changes. This was most likely another reason in February 2010 there was not a journal entry.

The Sandwich Generation

After Perry died the caregiving shifted to mom. I was now a midlife caregiver. I later wrote about this in a local publication called Natural Awakenings in December 2019. She lived with us in a three-generation household. It was mom, myself and my children. They were the bread, and I was "sandwiched" between them. I was in a traditional sandwich situation. I referred to a "bread" style as a robust "hard roll" having a well-formed crust on the outside with a soft inside. I had formed a hard shell from caregiving Perry for such a long time, but I was indeed soft on the inside. (See Appendix III)

Now we were focused on mom. As I look back to her last Christmas with us, it was the first time I could remember making cookies with her. I cherish that last memory.

A Daughter Not Caregiver/Nurse

Something I learned from burning out as a caregiver for Perry was that I could not do it all. I was not a superwoman. I could not be a functional full time professional, spouse, mother, and caregiver/nurse. Something had to give and sadly it did. Thank God, I learned from that experience and shifted my focus with mom.

I recall reading something from Dana Reeve, wife of Christopher "Superman" Reeve, after the equestrian accident that paralyzed him. She said she made a choice. The choice was to be his wife, not his nurse.

I made that conscious choice with mom; to be her daughter, not her caregiver/nurse. With that choice came no regrets. She moved into an assisted living apartment where she could get help from caregivers, and I could be her daughter for the remainder of her time.

2010-2011

Journal Entry

02-27-11, Three years ago this date died my love, my mate.
His spirit set free from a body sickly.
Gifts he sends down from heaven above to remind me of our very special love.
I smile and thank him with all of my heart.
For he was my true love right from the start.
Before each sunrise I see out my window a bright twinkling star.
I feel you so near yet see you so far.
What is that bright light in the eastern sky?
It's the planet Jupiter! I Googled it, I say with a sigh.
With each year that passes I miss you that much more.
The tears are not shed, the tears they do pour.

02-27-11
        It's 1:18 pm and I feel the warmth of the sunshine at that moment through the clouds. It warms me and gives me hope. To keep going and doing what you've guided me to do. Support the kids and finish school.
        I hear the snow melt and trickle down the drain. I feel peeks of the sun that warm my pain. Another year has passed

since the moment you were freed. More warmth, more sun is this the new sign? The suns disappeared and I'm out of rhyme. Onward we go with you safe in my heart and thoughts. Forever I'll love you, forget you NOT!

Dan is big now18 you have seen. Kat is no longer a teen. We all love you Perry you know it's true. Kat reminded Dan in his birthday card between the two. 15 &16 they were that day. Our love for you will never go away.

Mom did not last in her assisted living apt. for more than a week before a UTI sent her to the hospital. fast track to hospitalization for a colon mass and memory care unit with round the clock help before hospice.

Farewell to mom July 10, 2010 ☹

Facebook February 27, 2011
Three years ago this date died my love, my mate.
His spirit set free, from a body sickly.
Gifts he sends down from heaven above,
To remind me of our very special love.
Forever he has a place in my heart,
He was my true love, right from the start.
RIP Perry 57'-08'

Reflections......

I'm glad I did not miss another year of journal entry. A lot happened.

The Next Loss: I'm an Adult Orphan

My beloved mom died on July 10, 2010. She was my last living parent as dad died back in 1999. I did not realize it at the time I had just become what is coined an "Adult Orphan" until my education in Death, Dying and Bereavement brought it to my attention. An Adult Orphan is what one becomes when their last living parent dies. Mom was that last living parent.

A whole new type of grieving began when mom died. I immediately grieved her where with Perry, I delayed or dosed it. I let the grief hit me head on like a freight train. I allowed the pain in immediately and was able to regulate myself in about ten days. Mom's illness and caregiving was short compared to the marathon of Perry's illness. I grieved her, the friendship we forged in my adulthood and as a parent and the widow I had become. The kids grieved their grandma or "Babcia." Two significant loved ones in our household died within two and a half years. The kids were only ages 15 & 16 when their dad died and 17 & 19 when their grandmother died. Teenage grief was heavy in my house.

A Grandparents Funeral-Children Included

A couple of years before my father died, I took my son to the wake of an elderly person he did not know and was not emotionally connected with. It gave me the opportunity to introduce and answer any questions my young 5-year-old boy had before he experienced death in our own family. My father died a year later. Though he did not have a relationship with him, he was not afraid of the wake, funeral, and cemetery process.

Fast forward to 2010 when my daughter was 19 & son, 17 and the youngest grandsons, my nephews, were 11 & 7. My brother took the opportunity to make the wake a teaching moment for his children. They approached and looked at their "Babcia" lying in the casket. They were given permission to touch her if they wanted to and to ask questions. It was a beautiful teachable moment free of fear or anxiety that is sometimes projected from parents and other adults.

All the grandchildren were included in their grandmother's service. All the boys assisted as pallbearers wearing white cotton gloves. My son, the eldest grandson at 17, then 11 and the youngest of 7 wearing oversized cotton gloves for their age. The youngest stretching on his tippy toes to touch the bottom of the casket. My 19-year-old daughter sat in the limousine with the rest of us "ladies" and asked, "Could I be a pallbearer with my brother and cousins?" I responded with a resounding YES!!! Your grandmother would be honored to have all her grandchildren taking part in her departure. The eldest grandchild and only female pallbearer exited the limo and took her spot, proudly. It was an endearing display of love.

Yes, children can be included in the wake and funeral. It is highly individual and dependent on the child's ability to be in a potentially highly emotional environment. It is also dependent on the individual family customs and rituals. Each parent knows their child best and what they can handle. To be forced into an already uncomfortable and emotional environment can complicate an already delicate situation. They can be welcomed and included as long as the appropriate support is available if the need to leave becomes necessary.

Present in Her Own Way

As with my husband, I grieve mom's presence and her quirks. Holidays changed as she was no longer the elder of her siblings and glue that brought the extended family together. I am thankful my kids were old enough to have memories of her.

I grieve her birthday each year as she was only 80. I see her siblings having reached that age and beyond often wondering what she would have been like to attain the ages they are. I cry when I see their aging transformations and my heart hurts. I acknowledge her Angelversary with sorrow and reflection.

Mostly, I grieve with thanks. I am thankful for the gifts she provides me every year that her dark purple irises grow and multiply in my yard. The depth of the purple reminds me of a majestic ceremonial velvet cloak worn by royalty. She has gifted me with delicate purple Siberian irises and orange daylilies that attract dragonflies who grab my attention for a conversation. She planted the most beautiful periwinkle blue hydrangea bush that has a temperament subjected to mother nature's will in the summer month of July. It did not flourish in the summer of 2023 yet in 2024 it is bountiful and spectacular. Perhaps a sign from mom that this is the year for this book.

Thanks, mom, for always being with me and providing me with the gifts that keep on giving year after year. In honor of mom, I have been delighted to share the ever-multiplying purple bearded irises with friends for their own gardens.

2011-2012

02-27-12   1:18 pm
Four years ago this date, this moment you drew your last then feeling the loss of a love of more than three decades.
Once again I sit on our deck. I feel the warmth of this February sun. The sky is clear 51 degrees with a spring like breeze. Thank you for guiding me through the journey and completion of school. Thank you for watching over Katherine and Daniel. Please continue to guide us. Daniel feels and needs your love as does Kat. I sent Kat flowers to school today from you. I know how much you loved her.
Your presence was felt yesterday on Daniel's 19th Birthday. You dropped me a penny from heaven at Big Y. We went bowling. At the bowling alley they flashed track & field events on the score board. The pole-vaulter just like you was displayed many times. Just like you back in the day my memories were sound. And afterward we went to Tollis for pizza. Ryan was wearing a shirt from one of his cartoons Phineas and Pherb. The character on his shirt was "Perry the platypus." You were ever present 3x during our sons birthday. Thanks for letting me know you were with us.

Facebook February 27, 2012
    There was no entry. Did I really miss it? I have no clue how or why. This is just another thing that happens in grief. Forgetfulness can be blamed on "grief brain."

Reflections......

Graduated From School

Thanks to God, I completed my graduate studies and earned a Masters in Marriage and Family Therapy after a whirlwind 2.5 years of the hardest and different kind of work I had ever put into a college degree. Now it was time to gain further specialized experience and education in the world of grief and loss in directions which I could never have imagined.

A New Profession

Having now officially graduated, I was ready to hang up my shingle. I began prepping to open a therapy practice as a Marriage and Family Therapist specializing in grief, loss, and bereavement. I continued specialized education and bereavement support group facilitation to help increase my experience. I also began a 9-year journey of facilitating caregiver support groups statewide for the Huntington's Disease Society of America CT Affiliate/Chapter (HDSA CT). Giving back to the families with HD was part of finding my North Star process. I was able to do that because HD ended in our family with my husband's death. We did not have to

worry about our kids being at risk of this hereditary disease because they were adopted. That gave him peace in life and death.

Part Two
Years Five to Eight

2012-2013

Journal Entry

02-27-13 This has been the hardest month of February since you're gone. The energy is heavy, and my heart and soul are full of sadness. Dan is struggling. Look over him and send him love honey. He loves you and misses you so much that his heart breaks. Katherine has finally been able to open a little and admits the month of February sucks and she hates it.

I had my first dream about you a couple of weeks ago. I was with Maggie whose son Robbie had just died on January 13th. You looked so healthy and content. I'd say you were around 30-35. I guess it's true. We are whole again in heaven.

I know you are watching my progress in the therapy profession. I am struggling financially. Somehow you will make sure I make it. A few cutbacks are ok. I am low maintenance and simpler now.

I think you sent me a "GIFT" today. The receptionist at Flair For Hair said her brother married a Lithuanian woman. She is from Kaunas; the same town Kat and Dan were born.

It's 1:18 pm and I remember your very last breath. Shortly after, I see your essence, your spirit leave your body and ascend to the heavens.

Guide me into the future, my love, my Shrek. Keep us safe and watch us grow. Know that we are better people having been loved by you. If not for you, I would not be who I am past, present, or future.

Thanks to you, I live my life with the living. Thank you for giving me the opportunity to LIVE when I met you at 17 and married you at 19.

Forever yours

I'm posting a 5-year anniversary tribute on Facebook for the kids and myself. I want all your loved ones to remember how you were.

Facebook Post 02.27.13

At 1:18PM on this Date 5 years ago a very loved life died in my arms and joined the stars in Heaven. With a heavy heart and soul, I now go and reflect on that very time of the Great Love I once had. He was "MY SHREK", Perry Pausig. ♥♥.

Keep watching over us and sending your "signs" and "gifts". Loving husband and father to Kate and Dan.

Forever in our hearts and *souls*. They say in HEAVEN you are WHOLE and YOUNG Again.

Reflections......

Passage of Time

In my trainings, I have read that the first year of grief is the worst because it is the year of "firsts." And I have read the second year is hardest because it is the year of "permanence." As much as you would like to envision your loved one walking back into your life, they are not coming back.

I cannot erase 31 years of memories. The passage of time takes me to a music channel I recently found on Sirius XM called "The

Bridge." I love the music that takes me back to when we were just dating. Gosh, we were so young! Yet, some of those memories of yesteryear also remind me of just how much I have aged. As I write this, a memory from December 1977 came on that reminded me of when you were in angst, it was "Baby Come Back" by Player. It was a time another girl was pushing you to choose her over me. Thankfully, I WON! And our story continued.

Growing Pains

My reinvention as a grief therapist was experiencing its own growing pains. Marketing and self-promotion on a budget were challenges. Little did I know this was just the beginning of the growing pains associated with being self-employed. Financial struggles, belt tightening. I knew I could scale back and thankfully the kids felt secure. I knew we would eventually be okay.

A Strange Kind of Thanks

On February 8, 2013, came another blizzard to remember in my lifetime. Twenty-nine, I repeat "29" inches of snow almost consumed my inseam and beyond! The kids were in college, and I was left to my own devices to somehow get to our detached garage and get to the snowblower. What I thought I was going to do with its 18" intake height versus a 29-inch-high wall of snow, I had no clue. I tried to create a path. I managed to plow a single path about twenty feet from the garage. When I stopped, there was nowhere to turn. I backed up, put it back in the garage and went inside until I was dug out. A payloader needed to clear snow from the streets because it was impassable for the normal snow-plow.

It was the first time that I was thankful that you and mom were gone. It was because there was NO access out of the house to the street in the event of an emergency. There was no way help could have gotten to us if you or mom needed urgent help. I was alone, comfortable that I was okay, and the kids were safe at college. We had the Blizzard of 1978 in college, they had the Blizzard of 2013.

To Dream or Not to Dream

There was something that I was concerned about, that I never dreamt about him. Nor have I dreamt about mom or anyone else in my family I was close to that died. I concluded that there was no "unfinished business" with any of my close loved ones. I had the privilege of saying goodbye whether at their dying bedside or a brief time before. My thanks, admiration, final kiss, and fare-well were done, in their own time and it was right. I am eternally grateful for no "unfinished business" with my departed loved ones. My heart may be broken, it is not shattered.

Missing Words

I have learned that many people yearn for one last communi-cation with their loved ones who have crossed over. Mediums are sought after for questions unanswered. Sometimes answers are not found or what the seeker yearns to hear. So, they keep seeking whether it is "unfinished business," or a communication related to a sudden death by accident, other unspeakable tragedy, suicide, or murder. Others involve deaths out of the natural order of life. The death of a child, no matter the age, whether by natural causes, accident, suicide, or the unthinkable murder as the children who died on December 14, 2012, in Sandy Hook, CT create shattered hearts and communities beyond comprehension. I only pray that in time God will help them heal enough to get out of bed each day and breathe the best they can each and every day they live without their loved one.

I gained more exposure to bereaved parents by facilitating a support group for the Newtown Parent Connection from 2013 to 2016. These were parents who lost their children mostly to substance abuse. It was founded in 1993 and has grown into a compassionate venue for those who have lost a child or loved one due to substance abuse or catastrophic circumstances. Please look it up: Ctparentconnection.org.

Healing Self by Helping Others

Some people become advocates in the wake of tragedy as the Sandy Hook Promise (SHP) and Mothers Against Drunk Driving (MADD).

Three examples of incredible women I personally know have chosen to heal by helping others. One by using her gifts of sewing creativity, another by becoming an advocate for an incurable hereditary disease and the last by spreading words of kindness.

My dear friend Maggie Vitali uses her magical sewing skills to create incredibly special memory bears and other creations of love from a deceased loved one's clothing. She receives the fabric which speaks to her and guides her in specialized creations for her customers. I guess you can call her "The Fabric Whisperer." Moo Moo's Memory Bears is the name of her business of unique creations and can be found at Moomoosmemorybears.com. Moo Moo's Memory Bears was created in honor of her 31-year-old son, Robbie, who passed away in 2013 from a blood clot that traveled through his heart to his brain. In memory of Robbie, she donates 10% of the sale of each Moo Moo's Memory Bear to the National Blood Clot Alliance, stoptheclot.org. Maggie says, "Creating memories fills my heart with love."

Another friend, Kinser Cancelmo, has become a fierce warrior and advocate for both Huntington's Disease and Juvenile Huntington's Disease. Kinser's husband John died with HD as did Perry. The piece that skyrocketed her mission was when the juvenile form of inherited HD surfaced, ravaged and ultimately took the life of her 15-year-old daughter, Meg, in November of 2015. It would only be 3 months later when John died from HD. Juvenile HD is now affecting her last living child, 28-year-old Alyssa. Kinser knew and knows how to "fight" for her sick children. Kinser has taken her advocacy and speaks on the national level with the Huntington's Disease Society of America.

(HDSA.org) and JHD Advocacy & Meg's Fight For a Cure, JHD Foundation. She is a contributing author in the book "Life Interrupted, Volume 2: Living the unimaginable horror of what has been called the worst disease known to mankind, Huntington's patients and caregivers tell their stories "(October 2018). Her story was also featured: https://www.youtube.com/watch?v=nCJS64-dpbg.

And Jodi Walton creates "Kindness" rocks and shells to honor her 29-year-old son David who was killed in 2019 while working with the SC DOT. She leaves and shares them everywhere she can. She has a Facebook page called DAVID'S ROCKS. She began painting rocks as therapy for herself. Each painted rock bears David's name to which she knows she is spreading his love and kindness worldwide. She notes where they have been spotted on a pin map. This world has and still needs more people like Maggie, Kinser and Jodi to spread love, kindness and advocate for the causes of their loved one's deaths and others.

Hate Means...

Grief can bring emotions of hate. Hating one's life and its challenges without your loved one beside you. There were so many times I hated that you died, I hated being a single mother, I hated being the sole provider and I really hated trying to be both mom and dad. I could just and did scream! I hated making decisions alone. I hated always being the one in charge, the responsible one. You were gone, Mom was gone. Someone once told me "You are the captain of the ship; you must be strong!" There were days, and still are some, I wanted to be a simple "passenger," not the captain. I wanted someone else to make decisions so I could rest a bit. These emotions of hate ebb and flow during the grieving process. I have learned to have my little pity parties, which are short lived, and I carry on.

I recall back in 1996, a school social worker once told me, "Your child will say they hate you, do not take it personal. It only means they cannot deal with something at the moment." My daughter was 5 years old at the time so the first time I heard the words, "I hate you" from her, thankfully I was prepared. Now I get it. When I have my pity party of "hate" I am experiencing a moment of not being able to deal with something at the moment.

Gifts & Little Synchronicities

Gifts, little synchronicities, and signs are things that tug at the heartstrings of the griever. They are warm and comforting re-minders that the spirit world where you reside is just a moment away if we are open to receiving from the great universe of life. One of those "gifts" over the years since you died is the presence of a hawk. I have come to think that the hawk is you in spirit. It flies high enough to see the "big picture." Much like you were in life, silently present. And, when you wanted to say something, you would speak up, loud enough because it was important.

One day I was in the house and heard the loudest hawk squawk out back. I went outside and there he was circling and doing so until I acknowledged it, you, and then he flew off.

One year we had a hawk's nest in our back yard. Two young eyas's were born. I watched as their mom and dad tended to them; that was a majestic gift.

I often spot a hawk as I enter the ramp to the highway. A sign that my journey, whatever the distance, is being protected.

The hawk showed its presence, the strongest in recent history as it perched itself across the street from our house on a tree branch, then the telephone pole. It remained perched facing our house as if it were a sentinel, a guardian indeed.

On July 24, 2024, at 7:07 pm I received a gift that I will interpret as your blessing, to complete this book. I was sitting on our back porch and heard a thundering thump against the window. He clipped the window just enough to get my attention. I saw the largest wing flash by. Low and behold he perched atop the peak of our garage. I grabbed my cellphone and took a few snapshots of this beautiful creature. I call it a "he" because it is you!

He not only stayed there while I took grainy pics through the screened window. He stayed there until I got outside to take a clear photo. He looked forward and I snapped an elegant and regal profile shot. Then he turned his head and looked straight at me. I captured him as he looked at me! We met eye to eye as if the message he was sending to me was loud and clear. "I am here. I am watching over you. You will be okay. Continue on the path you are going." Once I confirmed I took the photo, I had a visceral reaction. I started shaking and crying that such a HUGE gift was just given to me by my love. The significant presence the hawk has in my life since Perry's death has me convinced that it is my spirit guide, the messenger from the parallel universe that Perry exists in as we travel together while we are apart. It was a sure sign that I am doing the right thing and moving in the right direction with my life and with this book. God and my North Star continue to guide me.

I have included a black and white cropped photo of this "gift" at the end of this Part Two section.

2013-2014

Journal Entry

02/27/14: 1:04 p. You know your boy turned 21 yesterday. Thanks for giving him a great day. Another year gone by and that makes 6.

A lot went as you well know. Work is still unsteady. I'm scared financially. I'm trying to follow my heart and the path you opened for me in this new career. Please continue to look over us as I struggle. Give me and the kids the courage and strength to keep moving forward.

It's cold and windy today. My heart misses your presence & your laughter & silliness when you were well. I thank you & God every day for sending angels to look after us and help. They are good souls and really care.

1:09p. I wish I truly knew how to be both parents because I continue to struggle being single. Please continue to help me help the kids grow and prosper. I too want to continue to grow & prosper. I don't want to lose what we have built. I am much humbler now.

I can still remember was I held your head in my hands & stroked your face as you were struggling to take your last breaths with you facing me. Dad at your head and Paul at your back. Permission to go.

My heart & soul is so heavy at this moment of writing about this passage of time.

The kids and I love you and hold you in our hearts. I know you are with us always.

I'm doing God's work with the church and want to take the position Sr. Mauryeen has trained me for. My private practice, Newtown Parent Connection & HD Support Groups are my passion.

1:15p. Please continue to inspire me as I begin writing the book. I am ready to complete this journey for you, me & other families with HD. Help me through the door of completion & publishing. It's time to give myself a deadline, maybe June 1st, 2014.

It's 1:17p and I'm going outside. I sit on the deck steps of this cold cloudy & windy day.

1:18p and a HUGE wind blows my hair, the trees & chimes. The time of your death has once again come and passed. May positive change come as these winds do.

With eternal love

Facebook-February 27,2014

6 years ago, this date I said goodbye to the physical existence of my love. Trapped in a sickly vessel his spirit was ready to be free. That evening, he appeared as a bright star outside my bedroom window and continues to do so.

His spirit lives on in those whose lives he touched. I am honored and grateful to have experienced his love that remains with me now 37 years. I am blessed and think of you today and every day. Thank you for watching over us. ♥Perry ♥

Reflections......

2013 was a big year. I pushed ahead to work hard to gain more experience and education in grief, loss, and bereavement. In college, I signed up at the suggestion of a professor and became a student member of ADEC.

ADEC

The Association for Death Education and Counseling®, (ADEC) The Thanatology Association®, is one of the first interdisciplinary organizations in the field of dying, death, and bereavement. Its 1,500 members include a wide array of psychologists, counselors, social workers, educators, researchers, hospice personnel, clergy, and volunteers. ADEC offers two respected credentials, which serve to enhance a professional standing and recognize expertise in the field of Death, Dying, Loss, Grief, and Bereavement.

My first step was to take the CT Certified in Thanatology exam. It is a foundational certification for Thanatology Professionals. The CT requires evidence of substantial related experience and thanatological education, as well as the successful completion of a standardized certification exam. I took the exam in 2012 and failed. Unfortunately, it is only offered once a year. I had a full year to prepare to take it again. Through perseverance, I took it and passed and earned the CT in 2013. It was a huge step in my path to becoming a bereavement professional. I was incredibly proud of earning this distinction as it later helped in my professional career.

A Book in My Future

Writing a book about our journey with HD was something I never would have imagined attempting. The seeds were sowed and sprouting began. It was a learning process and opportunity to create other authored publications on a smaller scale. See the Appendix Section in the back of this book for a sampling of those publications.

2014-2015

Journal Entry

02/27/15: Hey there, here I am again. It's 1:05pm. I'm on the deck steps & the birds are chirping. The sun is warm through the cold breeze. And the feeder is empty thanks to those dang squirrels.

It's been quite a year with Dan turning 22, my going to the HDSA Convention in Louisville, KY and spending the remaining hours of July-Sept. 26, Mom & Dad's BD writing & publishing our book.

It's in honor of you, An AffaiЯ Worth Remembering w/HD, Incurable Love & Intimacy During an Incurable Illness. I'm trying to get it out into the HD Community. Kat graduated from college & now Dan is 22.

Say hi to Gary S. & Alfredo G. Tell them we wives will stick together.

1:11p. Our Father, Hail Mary.

1:17p. 7 years ago I sat with you & Dad & Paul as you drew in and exhaled your last breath. Though I miss you, I am relieved you are "Free" you have guided me to do some great work in your honor with passion & purpose. I lost you long before death but not long enough to stop learning from you & this disease.

1:18p, I promise I will continue to help other HD families. Please keep opening doors. I am financially struggling please give me a sign that I and we will be okay.

Goodbye again the Love of My Life.

Keep sending me signs. Until next year 2/27/16

Facebook 02-27-15

Ok, I just wrote a long poignant dedication to you on this 7th Anniversary of your death. And "Poof" it disappeared because Windows decided to update. Perhaps this is your acknowledgement that "you got it".

Here is the "simplified" version. In this last year, thanks for watching over us, guiding us with your eternal Love and inspiring me to create "An Affair Worth Remembering With Huntington's Disease." We were and will always be a great team. ♥Perry 02/27/08 ♥

Reflections...

Sadly, two friends lost their husbands over the last year. One from a tragic motor vehicle accident and the other from cancer. I never thought I would be the first in my friends' groups to be a widow. More friends lost their spouses in the following years.

Financial struggles remain real as a widow, single parent, and a reinvented mid-lifer. It is another thorn that remains in the grieving process. Struggling, struggling, struggling but never giving up.

AAWR

The biggest leap of faith was self-publishing my first book. I felt compelled to give back to the HD Community and educate others with our story and I had experienced and learned.

"An AffaiЯ Worth Remembering with Huntington's Disease", *Incurable Love & Intimacy During an Incurable Illness*" was officially published in September 2014.

2015-2016

Journal Entry

02/27/16   8 years 1:00pm

I'm here again. On the deck steps. The sun is shining down on me and feels so warm through the cold February breeze.

This year, this month of February has been the most difficult and I don't know why. I seem to have a heightened sensitivity as the years pass. Seeing Aunt Helen at 85 makes me sad because Mom did not get there.

As you know, Dan got his driver's license. I'm saddened that the kids seem lost. I don't know what Kat's future holds.

Thank you for sending me the beautiful hummingbirds & butterflies to our garden last summer.

Thank you for sending "CHIP" the cardinal.

Thank you for sending me the beautiful hawks on a regular basis. I need these signs of nature.

Thank you for sending me to the HD Convention in Dallas, TX last year to present.

Thank you for giving me the inspiration to make the book an e-book. I hope the world of HD researchers, docs & therapists access it.

Thank you for UNH's recognition of Women's 40th Anniversary in Athletics.

Thank you for Dan D's gift to send the kids to the diner with me.

Thank you for sending me the angels to help me.

Please continue to send signs & care for me & the kids. I am struggling horribly financially, barely paycheck to paycheck.

Thank you for Sr. Mauryeen & the opportunities at the Mercy Center.

I hope the Adult Orphan series takes off so I can help myself & others.

I am studying for the CT MFT Lic exam. Taking it on March 19. Please help me retain the knowledge as I study & pass it so some more PT financial doors open. I need to be stable.

Now I close to pray and acknowledge your death in my arms, Dad's & Paul's on 2/27/16, 1:18pm.

Until next year. I'll be looking for you.

Love, Me ...

Facebook-February 27,2016

8 years ago today I felt your life slipping away. I refused to let you lay alone on your deathbed so I pushed you over making room for me, just one last time. You made it through our son's birthday and I thanked you. When your time came I held you and stroked your grey & blonde hair. I was witness to your last breath. You gave me the greatest gifts, a shared life, our children & everlasting love. I watched your spirit leave your body in a golden shimmer that drifted to the heavens. I knew you were headed home to be whole again.

Thank you for sending me signs in many shapes & forms. In spirit, I am never alone because you are there. Keep them coming, they are food for my soul validating my purpose & meaning. ♥♥

Reflections......

Mom Did Not Get Old Enough

Life continues to move forward if you let it, even during moments of resistance and trepidation. It does not shield you from grief that creeps up and slaps you upside your head on occasion. The example here is seeing mom's next in line sister turn 85. Knowing mom only made it to 80 makes me think every time I see one of her siblings that has passed the age of 80, what would she look like, be like? The what ifs occur after any age a loved one dies. Certainly, it is worse the younger a person is when they died.

Grieving Companionship in Aging

Grief over a spouse who has died also pops up when couples are seen together, aging together. Living into the "retirement years" we never had. However, if it is a commercial for an assisted living community, there is a good chance that the population is full of widows and widowers that are enjoying a second maybe third chance at companionship and love.

Rule-Out

Growing pains, financial and otherwise, have been a constant. God has given me the strength to persevere and look for possibilities. Creativity in my work has helped. I have a very tall pile of ideas that I tried. They included workshops, presentations, and various attempts at marketing. However, if I break down that down pile into successes and failures, the failure pile is much larger. I have chosen to re-frame the failure pile and refer to it as my "rule-out" pile. I am ruling out what was not meant for me to pursue. I tried; it did not work therefore I moved on. But not having first learned from the attempts. They are not really failures. They are simply test runs of ideas. The success pile is small yet sound having created a solid foundation to build upon. I think I would rather have it that way. The rule-out pile simply cleared the "weeds and brush" from the path I am on to become who I am today and beyond. What I uncover in the process are the pearls of knowledge and wisdom and gems of experience yet to behold.

A National Presenter!

I have made presentations on the local and state level since the 1980's when I was in police work. This was a different and exciting time of growth. In 2015, I was chosen to present to the Huntington's Disease Community at the 30th HDSA National Convention in Dallas, TX. I had the opportunity to present three different workshops. One to social workers and two caregiver track presentations. One of caregiver presentations was *Managing Marital Relations with HD* that was recorded and available on my website. The other was *Caregiver Burden: Six Essentials.* It was the first time I presented on a national level, had my book for sale, *An AffaiЯ Worth Remembering With Huntington's Disease*

at an HD event, and to be with so many people involved in advocacy, education and searching for a cure for Huntington's

Part Three
Years Nine to Twelve

2016-2017

Journal Entry

02-27-17 1:08pm
Dear Perry,
I'm here. In my spot on our deck steps feeling the warm February sun through the clouds. This month has been harder than usual. I don't quite know why.

It's been quite a year as last year this time neither Katherine nor Daniel had jobs. Now they do. I know you opened the doors for us last June.

Katherine at NHH&RC Baby sitting service. Dan at Shoprite. Me at the VNA. This job was certainly delivered to me via Cathy D. from you. I passed my licensing exam in March/April 2016.

As you see the VNA is good for me and I'm growing. So much!

Dan got his license and a scooter. This little truck had our sign on it with the blue butterfly.

Princess joined you on 9-29-16. It was so sad to see her wither. She taught me too to be with hospice.

Your Tubby is here with me now as I write.

Thank you for your signs, gifts & love. Thank you for sending me help which is good for all of us.

I wrote something on Facebook & will attach it.

Thank you God for caring & watching over us & giving Perry wings of freedom.

Until next year my Love……

February 27, 2017

Perry, 9 years ago today you joined the Lord to love and guide us from above. Today, with tears of gratitude and love, I honor your example of living and loving life.

I was recently told that we were soulmates in other lives than this one. And, that I emit a white light of healing. That light is you. The light of the love and life we shared and the light you left within me to grow. Grow and learn I have about this lifelong grieving process. Grow and learn I will continue to do as I witness, companion and work with others on their own process. Grow and learn the kids and I will do together because we were blessed to be loved by you.

Keep those "signs" coming, my eyes, ears and heart are wide open.

I will remember thee in my heart, my soul, and my mind.

Thank you for loving me. Thank you, God, for giving him wings to fly.

Robin W.A. ……………..

Debbie, I want to share with you...I always feel slightly heartbroken when I read your beautiful honoring posts...

And I want to thank you for helping anyone who reads your words feel lifted in this kinda sorrow. Because you chose to grow and learn from this and because you chose to celebrate his life it reminds me and others that even in darkest moments. Most painful loss.... And broken places... Light gets in through the cracks.

In my opinion, we don't do this alone... Guidance from above and words like yours from here. Is how we all survive. I think, although I did not know Perry, he would be very impressed with how strong you are. Thank you for telling us about him. And in sharing your poetic words which tells us more about you. Xo

Reflections......

My North Star Beacons, Again

Remember GPS? God's Positioning System. He was directing me to my North Star once again. I had taken and passed Connecticut's Licensing Exam becoming a LMFT, Licensed Marriage and Family Therapist. This licensing further cemented my credentials for professional advancement along with my already earned Certified in Thanatology in 2013. The conduit was my friend Cathy. She was a volunteer at a local Visiting Nurse Agency. Cathy was facilitating a bereavement group in a local church and invited me to co-facilitate on occasion. She told me a local VNA (Visiting Nurse Agency) was expanding their services and starting a hospice program. She directed me to their Caregiver Volunteer Coordinator, Jo Ann. Jo Ann suggested I interview for the Hospice Bereavement Coordinator position. I interviewed with my portfolio of credentials and workshops in hand. I was offered and accepted the position effective June 27, 2016.

Jo Ann became the Hospice Volunteer Coordinator, and I was the Hospice Bereavement Coordinator for VNA Community Healthcare and Hospice, now Yale New Haven Health-Health at Home-Hospice. Over the last 8 years it has been a great partnership! To this day we work closely in an effort to ensure the services we provide our hospice families and team members remain a well-oiled machine. A running joke I have with Jo Ann is that no one can say no to her. She is the perfect person for recruiting volunteers with her wisdom and incredibly beautiful soul that radiates wherever she goes!

Pet Loss Is A Loss

Pet loss is a loss that often goes unacknowledged. It can be an example of what Dr. Kenneth Doka coined as disenfranchised. A loss that is not acknowledged on a societal level because it is not significant.

Not significant? Ask the elderly person whose pet was not only their best friend, it was their daily companion, their "baby." I recall how my own mom grieved so when her beloved sheltie died. She enjoyed the company of her constant companion for over a decade.

My first real pet loss and home "hospice" of sorts experience was in 2016 with our cat named "Princess". She was the most beautiful jet-black feline whose fur was as soft as mink. She was petite and as royal as an Egyptian princess. We had her since 2000 when she and her brother, Tubby were 8 weeks old. Princess was just 16 years old when she started losing weight rapidly. She was an indoor-outdoor cat and within a weeks' time she died. I suspected she may have been exposed to poison while outside.

I recall holding, carrying, and tending to her during those life ending moments. Seeing her wobble from weakness was heartbreaking. Cradling her fragile body on my chest during those last hours surely felt like I was holding a premature baby.

Princess was the first of 3 black cats we had that died. Johnny was adopted from a shelter after Princess and Tubby. He died at 11 years old after an apparent stroke. Tubby, our guardian angel who captured Perry's heart throughout his illness with HD, died in 2019 at 19 years old. Each held a special place in our hearts and were acknowledged with pure love as they crossed over the "Rainbow Bridge" because they were truly heaven sent. Our pets can and often provide vital support beyond human connection and experience. Many tears have been shed on my cat's fur over the years from my childhood to present.

A few resources to check for pet loss can be found through your local veterinarian, online search, and social media. Pet lovers, the parents of fur babies can be easily found if you know where to look. One organization, the Association for Pet Loss and Bereavement. (APLB.org) is referenced on the SAMSA, Substance Abuse and Mental Health Services Administration website.https://www.samhsa.gov/resource/dbhis/association-pet-loss-bereavement.

2017-2018

Journal Entry

02-27-18: I spoke with Dad today and told him I was thinking of him with you today. I said "I love you Dad." He said "I love you too."

It's 1:08pm and I'm on the deck in my annual writing spot. Tubby is sitting next to me. What a fine day weather wise. The sky is as clear blue as your eyes. The February sun is so nice and warm and it's 52 degrees with a light breeze.

Oh, another year has flown by. Kat is 26 soon to be 27 and your Daniel is now 25. It's amazing watching them grow older as I just made a collage of us at 19 &21, 23 &25. Where did the years go? How could it be 10 years already?

1:14. Thank you for giving me the recent signs of 2/18, the HUGE Hawk that got my attention as I entered the side door at church. St. Frances Cabrini. On 2/20 the only cardinal I saw all winter got my brief attention at IDT a the VNA in Guilford.

1:16. You will always be with me in my heart & soul. Thank you for guiding me & us.

1:18. You are free once again. I feel your spirit in and around me. You will be forever remembered in the stories we shared.

Our Father...

Hail Mary...

Gratitude for what was and will be.

Until next year 2019, Love you Forever

Facebook 2/27/18

10 years ago today, yet at this moment, it seems like a day since you gained freedom from the imprisonment of Huntington's Disease. The death anniversary syndrome feels especially strong this year. Surreal is the passage of a decade. How could it be 10 years ago? How could it be 40 years since we climbed trees, snorkeled, and fished? True Love IS forever. You were my SHREK before there was one. So lucky am I to have had one great Love in my lifetime. Through God's guidance and your "signs", my life's journey continues on a path of daily enrichment. All because you loved me.

Reflections......

A Decade In A Lifetime

I began writing thoughts of this new book at year TEN, it was 2018, a decade since my whole heart, my timepiece was fractured when I knew the love of my life was entering the death process. Ten weeks later he died in my arms. Hours before he died it rained the tears of God calling him home.

Grief did not start at the time of death, for me, it truly started the moment my heart, my loving timepiece, shattered with the reality the end was near. And then, he was gone. The rain and God's tears stopped at my love's death.

The grieving of my love's death process began in 2007. It has been and will be a process for the rest of my life.

2018-2019

Journal Entry

2-27-19

It's 11 years today. I'm' not where I usually am on our deck looking at the sun.

It is actually cloudy & cold and about to start snowing. I had PT for my foot this morning & saw a hawk on Pool Rd. on the way home. Once home "Chip" the cardinal greeted me and "Girl Chip."

Today I write to you from Quinnipiac University Medical School Rare Disease Symposium. We are a Chapter now as of February. Sue McGann, Nicole Spencer & I are representing HD at a table.

Until next year my love. Continue guiding us and giving us hope.

Facebook February 27, 2019

At Quinnipiac University School of Medicine's Rare Disease Symposium with Susan B. McGann & Nicole Ann Spencer hosting our Huntington's Disease information table. Huntington's Disease Society of America, CT Chapter.

This was a great opportunity to spread HD awareness to the budding community of new medical students, nurses, and social workers, those who may encounter a person with HD and an HD family in their careers.

This is an appropriate event to be at as I honor the 11th Anniversary of Perry's death today.

Reflections......

Huntington's Disease Awareness Continues

Perry's death did not end my involvement with the HD Community. I knew entering the hospice community that we would have an HD patient. Whether I knew the family from facilitating HD Caregiver support groups for 9 years or not. I knew I could be a resource for HD families in hospice. To date, we have had two Huntington's Disease patients. We also have a nurse who is familiar with HD. Thankfully, my resources have been available and useful.

2019-2020

Journal Entry

02-27-2020

It's 12:58 pm and I'm at the Mercy Center in Madison. It's one of the most spiritual places that I have visited since you've died.

I walked the labyrinth and prayed for Dad, Katherine, Daniel, Paul & Lori.

It's 46 degrees and the winds are strong & the seas rough. Yet the sun on this February day is stronger and more spring like.

I did my first DEBRIEFING session with the VNACHC Hospice Team at the Guilford Community Ctr. It went better than anticipated. I feel supported by this special team and know that God sent me here. Perhaps with a little encouragement from you to keep doing good in honor of you.

1:02 pm. It's been a tough year as you know.

As you've seen, I'm working my butt off to raise my income in order to qualify for refinancing & debt consolidation.

It's time for the kids to keep growing. Dan, as you know, turned 27 yesterday and feels sadness every day because of your loss. Most especially at Birthday time.

Soon another year will be behind us.

I called Dad today.

1:10pm-This year seems harder than the rest. This Anniversary Syndrome seems deeper. My heart is heavy. I think I have finally realized that I have not grieved. I've been the captain of the ship since before you died and the last 12 years. I decided on my 60th BDay last November to really work on selfcare so once a month I go to Pam & get a Trifecta of Massage, Reiki & Reflexology.

On 7/10/20-7/12/20 I'm going to a weekend retreat at the Guest House in Chester-It's a spiritual-medium-intuitive retreat for the bereaved. I can be a passenger! Interestingly it starts on Mom's 10th death anniversary and ends on our 40th Church Anniv.

1:16pm Once again I hold you in my heart thinking about the last breaths you took with Dad & Paul on your side. Guide me God & Perry to my destiny & future.

Thank you for loving me and our children.

Until next year my love

Facebook February 27, 2020

12 years ago, today the love of my life died in my arms. So blessed was I to have experienced that one love that many never find.

I saw you today. I saw your spirit today in the sun that shined down on my face. I saw your larger-than-life spirit in the waves that crashed to meet me at the edge of the sand. I saw your heavenly hand stretched out from the sun-drenched water making a pathway to me.

I felt you today. I felt you in the unusual warmth of this February sun. I felt you in the strong winds signaling change was on its way. You lift up and spray sand at me to make sure I was fully present.

Our eternal love continues as you guide me from above. Our young love frozen in time, the love of a lifetime.

Reflections......

Have I Not Grieved?

Twelve years had passed, and I am now questioning whether I have grieved the death of my husband. Afterall, I am a grief professional. I am continuously educated about the grieving process. I cry, I journal, I remember, yet I question whether I put that education into practice on "myself."

One grief influencer/educator I follow and have many books from is Alan D. Wolfelt, Ph.D. In his book *Understanding Your Grief,* he discusses *"Dosing Your Pain."*

"Understand that you cannot embrace the pain of your grief all at once. If you were to feel it all at once, you could not survive. Instead, you must allow yourself to "dose" the pain — feel it in small waves then allow it to retreat until you are ready for the next wave." (pg.13)

Can you imagine the relief I felt to learn that I **had** been "dosing my pain" of grief all along, and still do? I have been putting my education into practice naturally on myself. Thank GOD!!!

If Yes, Then How?

I have just verified that I have been grieving my loss by dosing. The next question beckons, how have I grieved? That is answered by one of my next influencer/educators, Kenneth Doka, Ph.D. in his 2010 book with Terry Martin, *Grieving Beyond Gender: Understanding the Ways Men and Women Mourn.*

Dr. Doka cites three different grieving styles, instrumental, intuitive, and blended. I am going to offer the briefest distinction as this is not a textbook. **Intuitive** grief is experienced in waves of emotion, their expression mirrors inner feelings and emotions, there is more feeling than thinking, they are focused on exploring and expressing feelings and processing emotions. Society views it as a more "feminine "way of grieving. **Instrumental** grief is experienced in more physical or cognitive ways and is expressed in more physical, cognitive, or behavioral ways. There is more thinking than feeling. The focus is on doing and actively responding to grief. Society views it as a more "masculine" way of grieving. **Blended** grievers share the experiences, expressions, and adaptation strategies of both intuitive and instrumental grievers.

Aging To A Blended Griever

Once I learned about Doka and Martin's grieving styles, I looked at my own style of grieving. I learned something interesting about not only my style, but how it has changed in my own aging process.

We learn to grieve by what is taught to us by our parents or other elders. My family was not an outwardly emotional one. It is from my eastern European ancestral background. My mom was a nurse, a doer. My adverse childhood experiences taught me to be a doer. My first profession was in police work, a "doing" profession serving others. I am now a therapist and serve the bereaved.

I am a doer. I came to the realization that for much of my life I have been an "instrumental" griever. I am not masculine, I'm just a doer.

In 2011, I experienced an event that "broke" the stoic shell I had protecting me for so many decades. That, along with the aging process, has had a softening effect on me. I am noticing threads of an intuitive grieving style weave through the fabric of my instrumental grieving style. I have become more expressive and explorative in my feelings, and I seek comfort more often. I have evolved into a "blended" griever. My once stiff and sturdy duck canvas has become an embroidered piece of art. With that revelation, I am quite comfortable.

Part Four
Years Thirteen to Sixteen

2020-2021

Journal Entry

02-27-2021 Year 13

Hi, It's me again. It is that time of year I write. Perhaps this journey journal is the foundation of a new book-"Grief" An Affair Worth Remembering or something like that.

For some reason the last 2 weeks have been exceptionally hard. Certainly this last week has emotionally hit me hard. It's a visceral punch to my emotions evoking endless tears, a torn heart & inability to focus.

Only to be isolated indoors come March 2020 w/the COVID-19 Pandemic. The whole world was quarantined. Schools shut down on March 16, 2020.

Katherine's job closed & she has been jobless for the last 11 months. She had been cleaning Bunny's house & takes a lady, Mary shopping.

At 28 and almost 30 both are struggling, frustrated & stuck. It breaks my heart.

You have been visible as my hawk recently. Today 3 cooper hawks visited. Was it you, mom &??

It's 1:17 pm. Almost 1:18 pm the time you took your last breath. It is now 1:18. And I pray thanks & the Our Father.

It's rainy & cool as I sit on the veranda writing. Spring birds are chirping.

Thank you for sending help who continue to love & care for us. And comfort us in our grief & life.

Your Dad is hanging in there.

I just called Dad & told him I was thinking of him for you. He thanked me.

VNA-I went from 10 to 20 hrs in June 2020. New Director hopes for FT. I stepped down from the HD Board 12/31/20 & support groups, it was time.

Hospice is growing and I will complete 5 years in June, 2016-2021. I've been working remotely & from home Zooming since COVID-19.

I'm looking at selling our beloved Miata maybe May of 2021. My body is having a hard time getting in/out & comfort. It's time. It gave me great joy. Someone else deserves that joy.

Same time next year. 2/27/22.

I Love You Forever

Facebook-February 27, 2021 ·

Since this date in 2008 this beautiful creature (Hawk) has watched over me since you left your earthly body. He reminds me to see the "Big Picture"

13 years is such a passage of time. Days to a week before each anniversary approaches, my body experiences a visceral array of emotions.

The normal what would have it been like if..... crosses my mind. Huntington's Disease began its long slow erosion of you subtly at age 33.

Forever, I will remember you in our youth because that's the age you are in heaven.

Reflections......

Learning New Tech Tricks a La Pandemic

Very few good things came out of the COVID-19 Pandemic. My enhanced learning of technology was one of them. On March 11, 2020, the World Health Organization (WHO), declared COVID-19 a global pandemic. (www.cdc.gov).

I was contracted in the fall of 2019 to run a 6 hour in person training at the CT Women's Consortium in April 2020. It is a local nonprofit offering continuing education credits for the behavioral health field. (www.womensconsortium.org) I was all set to work the room with my PowerPoint presentation props, metaphors, and cooperative learning exercises. BOOM! The COVID-19 Pandemic hit and all in person training was put to an abrupt and sudden halt. I was notified by the CT Women's Consortium that my workshop would be the first live training via video conferencing. Quickly, I had to become familiar with, no time for proficiency, video conferencing platforms such as Zoom, Microsoft Teams, Skype and for my therapy practice, Psychology Today's "Sessions" and Doxy. I had to get the right equipment beyond a simple laptop; therefore, I invested in a decent webcam and external microphone. I found a cool boom microphone for this workshop. I looked like a radio DJ spinning vinyl for the airwaves only without the vinyl and adding video. Can those of a certain age picture that flashback?

I did not think I could pull off a full day, 6-hour, training behind a webcam, not seeing the participants or interacting with them. My typical training energy is conducive to interaction, participation, props, the use of metaphors, and cooperative learning exercises. This was a huge challenge for my presentation style. This was a one-way viewing. The participants saw me, I could not see them, their facial expressions, whether they were sleeping, doing laundry, or otherwise paying attention elsewhere. This type of live training was new to everyone. I was talking into cyberspace. I planned the best I could while sharing my PowerPoint presentation with the participants. I scheduled little breaks and allowed for questions and answers to be addressed during the lunch break. It was the most exhausting trial by fire into video conference training I could have imagined. Six hours was a marathon! As the years progressed, the one-way piece got easier. It is not without technical difficulties that are beyond anyone's control. There lies the grace that has been gifted universally. Also, the flexibility of a "gumby" I am about to address. The longest I have had to present via video conference after that was two hours; that is a walk in the park compared to six!

I continue to tweak my technology and skill set. I am pretty proud given that technology was never part of my background. I have engineers and computer science family members, so I guess it is woven, like an embroidery thread, into my DNA somewhere. I never thought I would dip my toes into this water. I have since jumped in the waters of video conferencing and am treading pretty well. At least my head remains "mostly" above water.

Be A Gumby

A history in police work taught me to stop on a dime, recalculate and reroute when dispatched to emergencies that were triaged in order of necessity. We did not have the computers or GPS- satellites, Google, Siri or Waze assistance of today to give us directions. We used paper maps, an Arrow Book Guide and good old-fashioned drive the streets to learn your areas. We learned to be flexible because we had to.

Those skills in police work provided me with a valuable foundation in flexibility. They certainly helped when I was a new parent and as my late husband's caregiver. Those two hats I wore required the most flexible 24/7 positions I needed to survive. I had the flexible green toy back in the 1960's named "Gumby". I also loved his orange sidekick horse, "Pokey." I am sure many of you had them as well. They were the ultimate wire covered flexible toy. I use them as examples today of the flexibility we must have to navigate the constant changes and challenges in life.

Time to Let Go of Things

There were things we had to let go of as his illness progressed. The scuba diving equipment, the motorcycles of our coupledom and youth. And then others as my own body aged through injury, repair, arthritis, and replacement parts. Goodbye ice skates, rollerblades, bicycle, and other activities of my strong and whole bodied youth. The last memory of our adventures was the 2007 Mazda Miata we bought for Perry's 50th Birthday. It was our last hurrah that would give me some final memories of our lifetime. Fourteen years later, it served its time with me. My replacement parts, not the cars, dictated it was time for it to go to someone else that would experience the joy of its Mazda advertised "Zoom-Zoom" ride. Someone who could bend down into the little car and exit with the same agility deserved the many years of joy that remained in it. It was sold to continue that legacy of joy in May 2021, just in time for some summer fun.

2021-2022

Journal Entry

2-27-22 1:00pm 14 yrs

I'm not home this year again. Anna & Angela have me distracted by taking me to the Garden show at the Convention Center in Hartford.

It's 2 yrs since COVID closed us down on 3-16-20. A lot has happened this year. Maggie moved to NC to be closer to Danielle. It broke my heart. I miss her so. I started working FT with the VNA Hospice on 7/21/21. I Love it. We are being acquired by Yale Home Care Plus officially on 5-22-22.

God I miss you & just can't imagine what it would have been like to see you at almost "65". I woke up this morning to see your star outside my bedroom window. Under it was a sliver of the moon. ☽.

The Ukraine is hurting. Please send hope to them with this Russian invasion. Find my paternal grandparents & pray for their homeland.

It's almost 1:18! Until next year my forever P, my <u>Love</u>

Please continue to watch over & guide us. Amen

Facebook-February 27,2022
14 years ago today, you rode the highway to Heaven. Thank you for continuing to be that star outside my window at wakeup; sending me your "Signs" & Godwinks and guiding me to where I am today. Forever my Love.

Reflections......

Grieving Geographical Changes

We also grieve changes in our lives. Changes in relationships, our own physical abilities, changes in jobs, even moving! Relocation of a loved one that occurs at times during the aging process creates a loss in one's heart. Think of the college graduate that now moves across the country or elsewhere in the world to pursue the career of their choice. They are away from their home base of their youth and beloved parents. Many of my peers have children relocated to NC, CA, TX, MA, FL, WA and other states far from our backyard of CT.

Then it continues, when our very own friends and family relocate. Some become snowbirds to get out of the north to enjoy year-round warmth during our colder months. Some make a permanent move to the warmth. Still, others relocate to be near their only surviving children and grandchildren. Their heart and soul have moved away. They move just to be close enough. Close enough to have a healthy relationship and be involved like the old-fashioned family they once were before the move.

Yes, I am admittedly very selfish having included this section. I am sure I am not the only one that has experienced this grief due to geographical change. It is nevertheless a loss. I grieved the geographical change of my dearest friend. Of course, I knew she had to move. I grieve the impulse to pop by her house which was only 10 minutes away. I grieved the spontaneous moments of going out to breakfast or dinner, taking a drive or a road trip or just being physically available when either of us wanted or needed a visit. It took a while for me to get used to not seeing her so frequently. It has been almost 3 years since she moved. A move that truly broke my heart. However, being a "gumby," I learned to adjust, and we have adjusted. Thanks to cell phone technology, we text on a whim, we videochat on our phones and, I cannot believe I am writing this, but thanks to one of the resources we all learned to use from COVID-19, we use ZOOM as individuals and as a group of friends! Though she may be physically and geographically far, we are still in touch as if we were home separated by that 29-inch snow Blizzard of 2013 and cannot get out of the house. We remain close at heart. For that I will be forever grateful. Now it is a quick plane ride or lengthy drive if we want to meet face to face.

Grieving The Imaginary "Would Have Beens"

It is difficult to imagine a person whose life stripping disease that died at 50 was soon to turn "65" in 2022 and in 2024, "67". And imaginary it remained. It is interesting as time moves forward, we reflect and say "They would have been….." Whether it is a young person or elder that has died, all "would have been" at some point.

I have friends whose parents that died well past 80 and some late 90's. All of mom's siblings have passed her last age of 80. Dad "would have been" 99, Mom "would have been" 95 in 2024. Heck, my grandparents "would have been" well into their hundreds plus, plus. However, I do not think about what my grandparents "would have been." It is because they were always old. I think it is my very own aging process as time passes that I remember my own parents at certain ages. I remember when my parents celebrated their 25th wedding anniversary. I remember when mom was 50, 60, retired at 62, 65, and 80. I was fortunate enough to celebrate my 25th wedding anniversary. And I have now passed 50, 60, 62, not retired, and can clearly see the billboard displaying a bold "65" through my "windshield" as I drive forward in life.

Another Peer Group Widow

No one is immune to death. As Perry died from complications with Huntington's Disease, another friend's husband died in a motor vehicle accident in 2014. In 2022, the death of a spouse to a third peer in a group of us moms who have been friendly since 1998-ish. This 71-year-old spouse died from complications with Alzheimer's Disease. After 26 years we have another thing in common, our spouses died. This was not the club any of us signed up for 26 years ago. That was as a Girl Scout mom, by choice. This time it was by circumstance.

2022-2023

Journal Entry

02-27-23 1:03pm
I drove to Jacobs Beach in Guilford from the VNA/HCP office to write. The biggest hawk flew to a tree on my way down to the shore. Was it you??

It's sunny now but we were supposed to get 6" of snow tonight on what has been a pretty snow free winter.

Work is good. I presented in Newport last May 13, 22. Kat joined me for the weekend. I took a BIG road trip to NC by myself to see Maggie. My first VACATION in 12 yrs! It was a Blast driving to Chincoteague & seeing the horses. We drove to the Outer Banks, we saw the Doobie Bros 50th Anniversary concert.

Kat & I went to an air show in NY to see the USAF Thunder-birds-First Class seating. We saw a couple of plays.

Galit and I went to Tanglewood & saw Earth, Wind & Fire. It was the BEST Summer in a decade!!!!

Daniel is still struggling on the job front. Please, please send him some guidance from Heaven.

Your brother Paul dropped dead last year. Take care of him-Marge is devastated. Dad is weak & broken.

Coming into year 15 has been the hardest. My heart has burned in the strangest way.

I think it's time to write a new book-How does the Freshman 15 (yrs) of Grief sound?

I think there is enough time & experience & knowledge under my belt now.

I Love you Forever

Until next year my love P...........

Facebook-2.27.23

15 years ago, today your life slipped away in my arms. With a golden shimmer you ascended to the Heavens and have watched over us since. The painful memories of Huntington's Disease that stripped you of your being have receded to memories of your seizing the fullness of life.

Today, and always, I remember the man whose life brought joy in life to us.

Forever in my heart. After your death, I dedicated my life to death education and counseling. Helping others in their grieving process has been my route of healing. The knowledge has given me a "sneak peek" into the grieving process so there have been few surprises.

It has not taken away the process and painful moments of my grief because the heart is still separate from the brain. I'm grateful for that because LOVE endures all the seasons. The heart helps me understand at the truest level, the process of grieving a loved one.

Thank you, Lord, for giving me that gift of a forever love.

Reflections......

A Growth Spurt

"Trust the Process" is the motto for Marriage and Family Therapists. We expect it from our clients and often forget it ourselves. I had been in the grief and therapy profession for 11 years.

I have taken many opportunities for growth such as local and Connecticut presentations which grew to live presentations because of COVID-19. The year 2022 took me to the regional level when I submitted a proposal to present at the New England Homecare Hospice Conference & Trade Show in Newport, R.I. It may have only been a breakout session, but I was there presenting on the next level!

I previously presented on a national level with the Huntington's Disease Society of America. I was a Marriage and Family Therapist then. It was before my work in hospice began. Now I do more presentations relating to death and dying, grief, loss, and bereavement. And here I am, about to publish a book on "grief."

12 Years to Self-Care

The last "vacation" I took was January 2010, before mom died. It would be "12 years" before I had the time, money and felt the emotional freedom to bust out and really have some fun. 2022 was a summer to remember. I drove down to my friends in North Carolina, closing that geographical gap to make some memories neither of us will ever forget. The solo drive reinstated a sense of wanderlust, adventure and freedom I thought I had lost. For ten days, I recharged my batteries tenfold. Because I am a "gumby," I adapted myself to a hybrid level of travel. I used both paper maps and the car's GPS. Yes, there were a few wrong turns here and there. That was part of the adventure, discovering new places off the beaten path. It was the "scenic route." One of the biggest challenges was where to seek shelter when a tornado warning blared over the radio. Thankfully, there was no tornado, and the trip was one for the books.

It was also summer to look to the skies! Top Gun-Maverick hit the theaters, and I had the opportunity to see, in person, the United States Air Force Thunderbirds. The Thunderbirds are the premier flight squad for the Air Force. On my bucket list remains to see, in person, the Blue Angels, the flight demonstration squadron of the U.S. Navy and its jets are flown by naval and marine aviators.

I traveled to places that I had never been, attended two concerts of my favorite bands, the Doobie Brothers and Earth, Wind and Fire, with people whose company I thoroughly enjoy. This summer was a turning point where I learned to have fun again. Truth be told, I am too old now to wait twelve years between vacations and self-care events. It is time to live. It does not have to be expensive. I had very affordable lawn seats at both of the best concerts I had ever attended. And thank God, we had great weather too!

2023-2024

Journal Entry

2-27-14 16yrs

Here I am. It's 1:16pm and the sun is shining & warm as I sit on the steps of our deck. I hear the plane heading to land at Tweed. I hear the windchimes.

Your Dad joined you last year on 4-14-23. I hung a photo of you and him in my cubicle at work. The two of you were well, whole and on one of your fishing trips. You are with your parents and brother now. So many of you to watch over us down here.

Something is different this year. I feel a shift. Kat just had a tooth pulled today and I am suffering w/my left knee awaiting surgery and a joint replacement.

I think I have been distracted by my knee pain the last 2 months.

I started writing my new book. The Freshman 15 16 of Grief. I hope to have it published by my 65th BD. Let's see what I can get done over the next 9 months.

Dan still struggles. He attended the H.O.P.E. Program @ St. Raph. Let's HOPE he gets a job. Until next year my love

Facebook-February 27 2024

16 years ago today I said goodbye as my fingers stroked your golden & silver wavy hair. As the tears rolled down my face you took your final breath. Moments later you were freed from the wretched Huntington's Disease and the sickly earthly vessel of a body which once housed you.

Free you became to travel in my heart and my sight to see abundant "signs" to comfort me.

16 years, how can it be? No longer us, no longer we, just I, just me. Sometimes it feels like a moment and other times an eternity. True Love transcends my love for thee.

Reflections......

They Have Joined You

The two men, Perry's father and brother have joined him. His brother suddenly died in December 2022 and his already fragile and broken Dad in April 2023. All three of the Pausig men are together again watching us from their heavenly perch. At least I know Perry (my hawk) has his nearby perch.

There are other elders that have crossed over in the recent past. My dear mentor, Sr. Mauryeen O'Brien died in August 2023. Elders that had a profound impact on our small "prayer group" or small Chrisitan community who meet for Bible study. Many years ago, I was one of 3 young, early 50 something, peers in the presence of 5 wise elders in the group. Two of the elders were retired educators with a wealth of knowledge we simply soaked up like a sponge. We met and sat in awe as their life and spiritual wisdom reflected on the readings. All but one died and we youngsters, now in our 60's grew by two and outnumbered the elders. The last of our five elders, Bunny, the mom to those of us who no longer had one, died in April 2024. I will be forever grateful for the gifts they shared with us during their senior years on earth. We are now the seniors, the elders. We have grown into the spot by age but somehow, I cannot imagine having their level of wisdom. We must find some "youngins" to help us feel wiser because we are definitely looking the part with our wrinkles of life experience and sparkling strands of hair.

Self-Care Continues

Changes occurred during this 16th year. It began as it usually does with my journaling. I expanded my self-care by attending two workshops by the amazing organization SYMI. Strengthen Your Mind Initiative (Strengthenyourmind.org). One was for current and retired first responders and the second for healthcare professionals. This is run by an incredible group of volunteers whose initiative is to work on resilience, inner strength, give you tools to lead life with a greater sense of meaning, purpose and connection, and help you release limiting beliefs and unhelpful thinking patterns that hold us back so we can be the best version of ourselves.

Drumming to the Beat of My Heart

Memorial Day 2023, my neighbor, Galit, introduced me to something new. Something that touched my heart and soul, spoke to my spirit, toned my arms, and affected, in a good way, those middle aged "batwings" on the bottom side of my biceps. DRUM-MING!!!! I do not mean the drums you see in a band, the kind that Ringo Starr played. Drumming as in "Drum Circles."

She shared an experience she had at a conference. It was done with an African drum called a djembe. She said there must be some drum circles available to us, so we looked on Facebook and low and behold we found one that met weekly right in our back yard only two miles away at a local state park. We watched some YouTube videos and were intrigued. We both bought ourselves starter synthetic djembes and joined the drop-in group down the street from us facilitated by a local fellow named Ken. We signed up for a few local Facebook groups that advertise drumming in CT. There was a lot to be had in our little state. At the moment we were content with remaining in our very closely located group and stayed within a 12-mile radius. The group was attended by a number of delightful drummers. Some were novices like us and others had been at it for up to 25 years. We soon learned and experienced the healing benefits of the drum vibrations, sound healing, and group play. Some brought all kinds of percussion instruments. All were happy to share their equipment. Some even traded or bought drums from others. This adventure continues.

I began to take a monthly lesson from another seasoned drummer named Mark who had trained in Guinea, Africa. Before I knew it, I was hooked. I went to a few full moon drum circles at a local beach and even danced around a bonfire! One night we saw a rocket that had launched from VA. Another night we saw a curious string of lights which ended up being a "Starlink" satellite, Elon Musk's spaceflight company, SpaceX. Starlink satellites provide coverage to dozens of countries through its 5,000 satellites. (cnet.com). Here we thought we were seeing a UFO!

Drumming has given me a great source of healing my mind, teaching me that I can play music, by ear, and thankfully without reading notes. I just love feeling the vibrations which are good for the immune system. www.drummingspirit.com/benefits-of-drumming/

I also have had the pleasure of receiving sound healing from another local artist, Jim from Spiritpercussion.com who introduced me to the Ukrainian tongue drum which to my ears soothes my soul and sounds a bit like a harp.

Fellow in Thanatology

It had been 10 years since I earned my CT (Certified in Thanatology) through ADEC.org. I thought it might be time to see if I had enough eligibility requirements to qualify for what would be the pinnacle of my credentials, Fellow in Thanatology (FT).

ADEC's FT® (Fellow in Thanatology) is an advanced certification for thanatology professionals. The FT® is awarded to individuals who can verify prior experience, education, and specified accomplishments in the field of death, dying, and bereavement and receive a passing score on the certification exam.

The FT was designed for more established professionals who have deepened their thanatological knowledge as well as a more expansive portfolio of scholarly and or professional experience within the field.

The requirements included: Master's Degree or Professional License, MFT, LMFT√; Prior Thanatology Experience of 8800 hours, I had 9100 hours√; Prior Thanatology Education of 45 hours, √; Personal Portfolio including 12 units representing specified past achievements/accomplishments, √;and Two recommendations from Supervisors or Colleagues, √. I was already a CT and was exempt from retaking the Certification Exam that applicants who were not CT's have to take.

I applied for the FT and was approved on August 14, 2023. I quickly shared a photo of my new credential with my mentor, Sr. Mauryeen, who was in hospice care in OH. I think her now being in hospice was the drive to pursue the FT. My sharing this accomplishment with her honored the support she has given me since 2008. It was prompted by the Lord indeed! I texted that it was the Lord's and my gift to her. She text responded *"This is truly a gift to me. And I am so proud of you. I think you and J. William Worden are on the same page now."* (Angel emoji)

Sr. Mauryeen died on August 22, 2023. I wept deeply when I realized all this was done "just in time." Thank you, God!

Widow to Widow-I finally fit In, Somewhere

Unfortunately, or fortunately depending on how you look at it. In my circle, I became the first widow. This was not a title I set to achieve by any means. The two women friends from a group I had been connected with since about 1998 lost their husbands. Gary, age 51, in 2014 and Carlos, age 71, in 2022. Their spouses Janet and Nancy recently joined a local widow's group in the summer of 2023. They asked me to come to their group as a speaker in November. I attended as a speaker, met the most amazing women whose husbands died at various ages from various causes and left as a new member of the group. A group I had been looking for yet not found. So many times, in life I have observed that our future can come from our past. This new connection came from my friends, those Girl Scout Mom friends from 1998. We have watched each other grow as moms and now as widows. Though we don't see or talk to each other often. We have a bond. And it only takes a phone call to re-engage that helping hand. This time I needed that help. Help to find a group of ladies who are moving forward on their own without their beloved spouses. This is to be continued indeed.

Traveling And Staying Connected With Family

I love to travel, especially if that includes my opportunity to drive, wander and discover. It expands my sense of adventure and wonder. It also gets me out of the house where I do not have to think about getting things done around the house. And that is another story in itself.

A bonus when traveling is visiting family. Especially those I have not seen for years, or decades. I recently chuckled when I visited a couple of my younger cousins who I had not seen face-to-face for about 27 years. My first thoughts were "boy you got old" clearly, I was not looking in the mirror at my own wrinkles and tinsel when I said that. It was a joy to catch up and continue.

The Sixteenth Holiday Season Was Different Too

For the first fifteen years of grief, I entered the fall/winter holiday season feeling the dread and sadness of my losses as they approached. It is that inner anticipation, not in a good way, that time was marching forward without my loved one. That feeling passes when the date/birthday/anniversary/holiday passes. It is called the "Anniversary Syndrome." For some strange reason, this year I did not feel its intensity. Not on my birthday, not on the anniversary of adopting our children, not on what would have been our 45th wedding anniversary. I acknowledged them with some cathartic written thoughts as usual as well as my trip to the cemetery. But this year, the hole which usually opens and looks to swallow me did not. Could my heart have created enough scar tissue around its broken wound where it did not hurt so much anymore? Or am I doing enough in my life to finally feel the heal? Was this the year of true healing? The sign came on Christmas Day 2023. It was a warm 50-degree day in Connecticut. I saw a beautiful red cardinal pecking on the ground in the wilted dried summer flower garden. I went outside to see it and it flew into the woods. I looked up into the leafless trees and there you were. My sign, your sign, the hawk. Looking at me. I snapped a photo with my phone. I thanked it (you) for visiting me on this quiet day. And, as it usually does, it flew off, its typical response after my acknowledgement. I wrote a caption on that photo "Merry Christmas Darling 2023". Tears are streaming down my face as I type because this beautiful spirit animal is what has connected us between our parallel planes. We still are walking together only yours on the other side and mine in life. The two strongest signs of your spirit reside in the hawk that follows me on my travels and oversees me in our back yard and the bright star that greets me every clear morning in the east sky. When you died that star appeared on February 28 as I awoke before sunrise. And on every clear morning since. I often wake up before sunrise year-round, so I do see it whether it is still pitch-black outside or just as the sun is at the eastern horizon. I had been mistaken in the past thinking that was the planet Jupiter. According to NASA.gov, that beautiful bright star, planet is VENUS!

Fyodor Dostoyevsky wrote, *"The mystery of human existence lies not in just staying alive, but in finding something to live for."*

That something is me. I want to live and go on living, learning, discovering, exploring, and experiencing the possibilities that await and are right for me. God has provided my North Star guiding my journey through life without Perry in this plane of physical earthly existence. Continue guiding me to the adventures that are still yet to behold in this life.

I look for guidance and direction both outwardly and within my heart's passions. This is my personal journey as the answer lies within me under all the layers of life that hide and sometimes complicate the journey.

Replacement Parts

What would a book that includes the aging process and sometimes grief of aging be without addressing our own health? We survived menopause. We endure annual mammograms, ultrasounds and pap smears. We are old enough for colonoscopies, Woo Hoo! We are old enough to feel the snap, crackle and pops of arthritic joints tamed by healthy eating, supplements and cortisone shots to relieve inflammation. We are also old enough to feel the wear and tear of the activities and sports that we took part in our youth. We are now requiring "replacement parts."

I know of a woman that has already had "3" joint replacements. She has a shoulder that is 18 years old, a hip that is 9 years old and a brand-new bouncing baby knee that is 7 weeks old. She even created a car wash type "punch" card and showed her surgeon in hopes that one future joint replacement might qualify as "FREE!" Just imagine if those replacement parts were children, one is a senior in high school, one is pre-adolescent, and the other is a newborn infant. That, my dear reader, is quite a range and perspective. What a busy and tired mom she would be.

Be kind to your aging joints. As we enter the Summer 2024 Olympics in Paris, France, I cannot help but take note of my current viewpoint. When I was a teen and twentysomething athlete, I would watch in awe! Now I not only watch in awe, but I also think, in forty years "that" one is going to need new hips, "that" one, new shoulders, and "that" one, new knees. In the meantime, I cheer on the evolving talents of the young who deserve to be recognized as the BEST in their sports. God Bless them all!

Lessons Learned

Over these last Freshman 16 years of Grief and cumulatively over the last near six and a half decades, I have a few takeaways. These are certainly not exhaustive but are in the forefront of my thoughts during this writing.

UBUNTU- "A person is a person through other persons." Or "I am because of you." as referenced by Archbishop Desmond Tutu in the Book of Joy by he and His Holiness the Dalai Lama (2016). It is because of God, my husband and so many others that I have experiences within this life, and I have become who I am. Through both the joy and suffering together we are able to keep moving forward. Because of "you" all of the people in my life. You have taught me ways to cope in life, and death, and provide the support I need.

"BE GOOD TO YOUR GIRLFRIENDS" by Yetta. This was a statement that stuck with me. About 2 years before COVID-19, I was a host "Girlfriend" on a public TV show called "Got

Girlfriends?" It was a group of women friends that had a passion to help others by sharing knowledge and experience and gained more by the special empowering stories provided by their guest "girlfriends." Peaches, Jan, Kim, and I were the hosts at that time. One of our guests was Yetta who made that statement. It was a powerful takeaway. Our tribe of women contribute and provide what no one else can.

FACETS IN A GEMSTONE- I cannot express how in my lifetime the number of friends has become individual facets in a yet to be complete gemstone. Alone, that person or facet is a cut in that gemstone. Cumulatively, those facets create the most beautiful gem of all. A representation of all that my life has encompassed. The gemstone represents my tribe of friends who have helped shape who I am and yet to be.

ANOTHER GEMSTONE-I would be remiss if I did not note another gemstone in my life that began its formation eight years ago; the hospice team to which I belong. Each and every member of that team is a facet to the gem that creates a team of caring individuals "called" to serve the patient and families at the end of life and after the death of their loved one.

Also, included in the hospice family of gemstones are my colleagues in the National Hospice and Palliative Care Organization's Bereavement Steering Committee. (NHPCO) I became a member of the steering committee three years ago. To say I am merely blessed to have other peers in bereavement is an understatement. I have learned from their depth of knowledge and contributed as well. This nationwide collective of resources from hospices that range from large to small in size is priceless.

I am truly blessed and possess great wealth beyond any monetary means having all this in my life. I hope my readers look within themselves and around to find theirs as well.

My Biggest Professional Influencers

I own about 300 books related to grief. These are my biggest professional influencers in my current work.

The late, Sr. Mauryeen O'Brien, O.P.
Dr. J.William Worden (Grief Counseling and Grief Therapy)
Dr. Kenneth Doka (DrKenDoka.com)
Dr. Alan Wolfelt (Centerforloss.com)
Dr Robert Neimeyer (Portlandinstitute.org)
David Kessler (Grief.com)
ADEC-Association for Death Education and Counseling
        (ADEC.org)
NHPCO Bereavement Steering Committee (MyNHPCO.org)
Hospice Foundation of America (Hospicefoundation.org)
Whatsyourgrief.com
and
Huntington's Disease Society of America (HDSA.org)

Epilogue

During these "Freshman 16" years of grief, I have become like a piece of Kintsugi pottery. Kintsugi pottery is the Japanese art of repairing a piece with gold or silver lacquer and understanding that the piece is more beautiful for having been broken. In this book I have written about my brokenness and journey into healing. My broken heart is depicted on the cover of this book and the next page showing the repaired cracks. Perhaps it is reinforced and now stronger with the love and experience that I have received during this process.

Am I more beautiful for having been broken? I'm not quite sure of that. I know having been broken by the loss and grief of the love of my life and adjusting to the aging process over the last 16 years without him have certainly changed me in many ways. My heart is more golden, and my hair is more silver. My wrinkles and scars show that I have lived, loved, experienced, and aged. I am softer, bolder, wiser.

Looks like I am ready to advance to the "Sophomore years of Grief," however many that will be. One thing is for sure. I will have graduated as a Senior in grief when I am once again reunited with my love, and we walk together on the same plane. PLEASE let that not be for a long, long, long time!

I still must advance through my Sophomore and Junior years and write those sequels to this book. Those years will be less in time because if those 3 take 16 years each to experience, that's another 48 years to live and that, my friends, is just not happening. I have more to do and more to offer readers like you. Only God knows when I will be ready to "graduate"; let's hope I continue to be a good student and earn my "credits" or be "retained" on this earth for a while longer so I can continue to learn.

In the meantime, look inward, it might be time to explore and discover your very own North Star.

Debbie

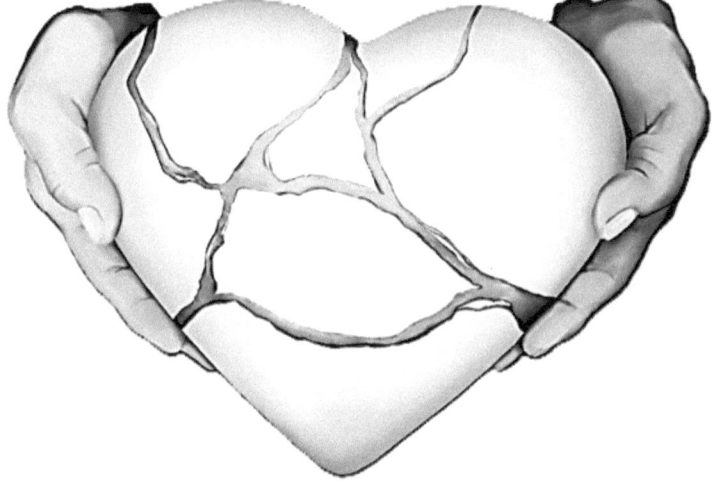

Introducing Nina Ciarleglio
Artist & Designer

Nina Ciarleglio is a bright and upcoming student and senior at Paier College of Art in Bridgeport, CT. I was introduced to Nina's work by her aunt as she shared, with immense pride, the amazing talent of her young adult niece. I thought, this book needs to be kicked up a notch with artwork beyond my simple means. Nina and I met and voilà! She created a draft of this book cover from my cell phone photo with the speed and tenacity that only a person of her young tech-savvy generation could do. A few swipes and clicks of the mouse and before I knew it the first draft was born. The finished product proved to be beyond my expectations as she captured the metallic shine of the gold repaired cracks.

Thank you, Nina, for agreeing to take on this project. I am proud to show the world this tiny preview into your no doubt boundless talents. May your senior year and subsequent graduation be a springboard into the future you are destined to have.

APPENDIX

I: Grieving Behind the Badge:
  We are the First Responders-Reflective Article
ADEC Forum Quarterly Publication of ADEC.
WWW.ADEC.ORG
Vol. 39, No.1- January 2013, pgs. 18 & 24

II: A Forever Bond: Connected in Life and After Death
  "It's All About LOVE"
Natural Awakenings, New Haven/Middlesex
NaturalNewHaven.com
August 2019 pgs. 32-33

III: The Sandwiched Generation:
  A Tale of Midlife Caregivers
Natural Awakenings, New Haven/Middlesex
NaturalNewHaven.com
December 2019 pgs. 30-31

IV: Grief Amplified + Mourning Interrupted
  =Mourning COVID-19 Style
Trauma Matters Special Edition: COVID-19 Summer 2020
A publication by the Connecticut Women's Consortium and the
Connecticut Department of Mental Health and Addiction Ser-
vices in support of the Connecticut Trauma and Gender
Initiative. www.womensconsortium.org

V: Will I always feel this bad during the Holiday Season?
  There is Hope with these 23 tips
2023 update Debbiepausigmft.com

VI: Thriving to Surviving with Six Essentials
2023 update Debbiepausigmft.com

APPENDIX I:

Grieving <u>Behind</u> the Badge: We are the First Responders
Reflective Article: Grief and Families
ADEC Forum Quarterly Publication of ADEC.
WWW.ADEC.ORG
Vol. 39, No.1- January 2013, pgs. 18 & 24
By Deborah Pausig, MFT, CCTP

As I heard the News Break of the shooting in Newtown, CT on 12/14/12, my thoughts immediately went to a place of muscle memory. That memory was 25 years of police training in another town in Connecticut. The First Responders are the Police, Fire and EMS who, by nature of their job, must respond, take control, protect, secure, give comfort, and find answers to tragic and traumatic situations such as Sandy Hook. These men and women must work with the utmost professionalism on the outside, while on the inside, there is "grieving behind their badges." Their hearts also break for the victims, families, and community they serve. It is not uncommon for First Responders to work and live in the same community. Imagine the identification they may have with the victims and their families. They shop at the same grocer, attend the same church, meet at the neighborhood coffee shop, attend little league games, participate in community events, and even have kids that attend the same school. As a First Responder called to Sandy Hook Elementary School, the searing thought of "It could be my child" or "someone I know is there" is racing through their own hearts. Yet, they respond and perform as trained professionals.

It is often forgotten that these professionals we so depend on for strength when we are weak, direction when we are lost, control in chaos have forever been impacted by this event. An event such as Sandy Hook can manifest in emotional, physical, cognitive, and interpersonal reactions in the lives of the First Responders. Emotional reactions can include terror, irritability, intense sadness/grief, and emotional numbing. Physical reactions can include fatigue, exhaustion, insomnia, hyper-arousal, and decreased appetite. Cognitive reactions can include impaired concentration, impaired decision making, memory impairment, nightmares, and intrusive thoughts/memories. Interpersonal reactions can include relational conflict, reduced intimacy, social withdrawal, and impaired work performance. (Zeefe, L, 2010)

Who do the First Responders reach out to? Assistance for the investigative portion of this incident came from local, state and federal law enforcement agencies. Another support function showed its presence. The Brotherhood of officers from towns around Connecticut volunteered their time to assist the Newtown officers with traffic control and anything else that was needed. I drove through Newtown the Sunday before Christmas. I felt the heaviness in my own being as my car inched past the endless memorials nearing its center. Traffic was crawling. People were walking great distances into town carrying flowers and small stuffed animals. Stopped in traffic, I saw an officer from Norwalk directing traffic. I thanked him for being in Newtown to help his brother officers. He asked if I was from Newtown. I responded, "No, I am a retired officer and current therapist." We shook hands and smiled as we parted. According to a study of disaster workers assigned to the World Trade Center (Crenshaw, 2007), a significant portion of disaster workers will not utilize mental health services even when readily available. (Jayasinghe, Spielman, Cancellare, Difede, Klausner & Glodean, 2005)

Father John Gatzak of the Office of Radio and TV for the Archdiocese of Hartford, CT, called me to join him on live radio, WJMJ-FM, on 12/27/12. We spent 1½ hours "ON THE AIR" talking about grief and the holidays, addressing the Newtown tragedy and reaching out to the First Responders. Hailing from the police culture, I know the importance of peer support and see its presence. Beyond that, therapists such as me are honored, available and willing to serve those that need us to work with the "grieving behind their badges."

Bibliography
Crenshaw, D. (2007). Chapter 29: The Family, Larger Systems, and Traumatic Death. In ADEC, Handbook of Thanatology (p. 289). Northbrook: Routledge.
Jayasinghe, N. S. (2005). Predictors of treatment utilization in World Trade Center attack disaster workers: Role of race/ethnicity and symptom severity. International Journal of Emergency Mental Health, 7, 91-100.
Zeefe, L. M. (2010, March 24). Responding to Traumatic Grief & Loss in the Aftermath of a Catastrophic Event, 9. PESI CE Study Package # ZHS041985. Eau Claire, Wisconsin, US: PESI, LLC.

Deborah Pausig is a Marriage and Family Therapist, Certified Clinical Trauma Professional, ADEC member since 2010 and a 25-year retired police officer from North Haven, CT. She holds a B.S. in Criminal Justice, a Master's Degree in Public Administration and a Master in Family Therapy Degree. She is a Bereavement Facilitator and Facilitator Trainer with the Family Life Office, Archdiocese of Hartford, CT, and a professional support group leader for the Huntington's Disease Society of America-CT Affiliate. www.debbiepausigmft.com.

APPENDIX II:

A Forever Bond: Connected in Life and After Death
"It's All About LOVE"
Natural Awakenings   New Haven/Middlesex
NaturalNewHaven.com, August 2019 pgs. 32-33
By Debbie Pausig, LMFT, CT

Life, Love, Death. It is chronological. It is linear. Yet it is not finite. The Bond with a loved one after death is indeed "INFINITE."

Ask the person who's "love of their life" died in their arms, saw their "spirit" leave their body and ascend into the universe to find "their" place in the stars outside their window, every night. They are the hawk at the entrance ramp of the highway guiding the days journey. They are the street sign with their name; initials that appear; number combinations that pop up; the name on your caller ID.

Ask the mother whose child died, no matter the age, about the hole in the center of their being, whose energy manifests in synchronicity with a "special" feeling…

Ask the adult child whose elder parent and "best friend" appears as an angel in cloud formation.

And, what about the feathers, pennies from heaven, songs, birds (cardinals, hawks, hummingbirds), animals, butterflies, dragon flies, moved objects, recipes, books that appear out of nowhere and so many more examples?

If you speak about these things to a person who has not experienced the profound death of a loved one, they look at you like you have "3 Heads!" They don't understand.

In "Hello from Heaven", (1995) Bill and Judy Guggenheim researched the field of After Death Communication confirming that life and love are eternal. They identified twelve most frequent types of after-death communication people report having with their deceased loved one. They are: Sensing a presence; Hearing a voice; Feeling a touch; Smelling a fragrance; Visual experience; Visions; Twilight experience; Experience while asleep; Out-of-Body experience; Telephone call; Physical phenomena and Symbolic experience. (www.after-death.com)

In her book "The Invisible String", (2000) Patrice Karst created a simple story for children and adults alike that "people who love each other are always connected by a very special string made of love. Even though you can't see it with your eyes, you can feel it deep in your heart and know that you are always connected to the ones you love." Though this was not specifically written with connecting with a loved one after death, its intention was to calm a child's fear of being apart from the ones they love.

In "Tuesdays with Morrie", (2005), Mitch Albom quoted Morrie Schwartz, "Death ends a life, not a relationship. All the love you created is still there. All the memories are still there. You live on-in the hearts of everyone you have touched and nurtured while you were here."

What connects you to a person that died? It's relationship and love. It's All About LOVE! This is not romantic love, nor hedonistic wanting and desire perceived as love. This is a deep-caring connected love that transcends time, and death. It is a forever love that was created in life that continues after death. It is a forever and continuing bond.

In recent times, memorials are posted on social media platforms such as Facebook to connect the memories and photos of a dead loved one to the living. This type of online mourning and connectedness give comfort to those left behind. Many photos of "signs" are posted that give the bereaved hope that the bond of love continues.

Others may find journaling, poem writing, song writing, even authoring a book, very cathartic. Creating a special email between the bereaved and deceased to share in cyberspace is another way to maintain communication, even though it is one way. The use of all these mediums can be of great comfort as sorrow is put into words.

Did you happen to see the lady who was talking to a dragon fly perched atop an orange Daylily? That Daylily was planted by her now deceased mother. It was quite the conversation. The woman carried on swearing her deceased husband was connecting with her through the dragon fly, which nodded its head, as she spoke into its eyes only 3 feet away. After all, dragon flies are transitional creatures. The woman chuckled and said if there was a "squirrel cam" atop the telephone pole across the street capturing this one-way conversation, she would have been taken away!

We indeed are and will always be connected by an infinite invisible string, our loved ones are in our hearts and our memories. We continue to share stories that came from generations before. We create new stories in the name of our loved one. Tell a story about your loved one......

We have forged A Forever Bond: Connected in Life and After Death. "It's All About LOVE"

Debbie Pausig, MFT, LMFT, CT is a Licensed Marriage and Family Therapist and Certified Thanatologist, Grief Counselor, National Speaker, Workshop Presenter, Huntington's Disease Support Group Facilitator, Bereavement Facilitator Trainer and VNA Community Healthcare & Hospice Bereavement Coordinator. She is the Author of "An Affair Worth Remembering with Huntington's Disease".
North Haven, CT.   www.debbiepausigmft.com

APPENDIX III:

The Sandwiched Generation:
A Tale of Midlife Caregivers
Natural Awakenings New Haven/Middlesex
NaturalNewHaven.com, December 2019 pgs. 30-31
By Debbie Pausig, LMFT, CT

"The Sandwich Generation" is a well-recognized term derived from caring for one's aging parents and their own children at the same time. It was first coined in 1981 by Social worker, Dorothy Miller who originally referred to younger women in their 30's-40's taking care of both their children and parents.

Which "sandwich" are you, the single, the double or triple decker? Perhaps, a more accurate question is what type of bread is your sandwich made of? "Flatbread" with a thin support system on each side? "White bread", a familiar staple of childhood, susceptible to getting mushy from external and internal sources. Or, a robust "Hard Roll" which has a well formed crust on the outside and is soft on the inside. How well do you stand up to the challenges of being "sandwiched" in between two age groups?

The Pew Research Center (1/30/13) published "Rising Financial Burden for Middle-aged Americans" (aged 40-59). Nearly 47% of adults in their 40's and 50's has a parent age 65 or older and are either raising a young child or financially supporting a grown child (age 18 or older). In "The Boomerang Generation" (3/15/12), the older of the children, 25-34 are approximately 29% of young adults who live with their parents. The parents of these young adults are being held responsible to care for their children longer than expected.

Carol Abaya, an expert on the sandwich generation, aging and elder/parent care issues defines three types of "Sandwiches":
Traditional: those sandwiched between aging parents who need care and/or help and their own children.
Club Sandwich: those in their 50's or 60's, sandwiched between aging parents, adult children and grandchildren, OR those in their 30's and 40's with young children, aging parents and grandparents. (Term coined by Carol Abaya)
Open Faced: anyone else involved in elder care. (Term coined by Carol Abaya) (www.sandwichgeneration.com)
We can commonly identify a familial generation average being 25 years. However, a current norm is delayed parenting where families are started in mid-30's. We see increased life span as a result of advances in medical science, healthcare and technology. Just picture this multilayer sandwich divided between 25 years: 100,75,50,25,1. Yes, 5 living generations could be present within a family. Today, more Baby Boomers are not only sandwich generationers, they are seniors themselves and experiencing their own health challenges. This begs the questions, who is taking care of who and what is involved in this care?

Challenges to those "sandwiched" can often include caregiving (physical) and financial support to both the elder and younger on each side. Then there is added need for emotional support. This can result in caregiver stress, burnout, depression, isolation, guilt and financial hardship. Personal time and time with one's partner become challenged. Time for the "fun stuff" such as hobbies, relationships and selfcare become a challenge. The "sandwiched" persons health and career status and/or opportunities are affected. There is a great strain on the "sandwiched" persons mental, emotional and physical health.

Where to go and what to do?
https://uwc.211ct.org/area-agency-on-aging/
Local caregiver support groups
www.caregiver.com

Caring for YOU, the Sandwiched One:
Be kind to yourself
Drink Water
Be spontaneous
Give yourself permission for a break
Drink Water
Take a walk
Eat a healthy snack
Drink Water
A little mindfulness goes a long way
Meditate using an App like "Insight Timer"
Drink Water
Carry a "Me Bag" including lotion, lip balm, water, a
journal, a novel, anything soothing for you.
Laugh at yourself, laugh with others.
Drink Water
Ask for help
Know "Go-To Peeps" for support
Seek Counseling/Therapy with someone who works with lifecycle transitions, caregiving, etc.
....
Caregiver burnout is not an option. Help is only the turn of a doorknob away. (Or call, text, email) You need only open the door to see help on the other side. And there are many people waiting to be asked.

It is truly an honor and privilege to witness and be part of our loved one's aging on one side and growth on the other. Who do you want to be, mother/father/daughter/son or a burned-out over-cooked piece of sandwich meat? It is a choice. There are plenty of useful and legitimate resources on the internet. It will help you enjoy your time with your family and allow you to be you without losing yourself. Perhaps the robust "Hard Roll", a well-formed crust on the outside and soft on the inside is the just right kind of sandwich bread to be.

Debbie Pausig, MFT, LMFT, CT is a Licensed Marriage and Family Therapist and Certified Thanatologist, Grief Counselor, National Speaker, Workshop Presenter, Huntington's Disease Support Group Facilitator, Bereavement Facilitator Trainer and VNA Community Healthcare & Hospice Bereavement Coordinator. She is the Author of "An Affair Worth Remembering with Huntington's Disease". North Haven, CT
www.debbiepausigmft.com.

APPENDIX IV:

GRIEF AMPLIFIED + MOURNING INTERUPTED =MOURNING COVID-19 Style
Trauma Matters Special Edition: COVID-19,
Summer 2020
A publication by the Connecticut Women's Consortium and the Connecticut Department of Mental Health and Addiction Services in support of the Connecticut Trauma and Gender Initiative.
www.womensconsortium.org
By Debbie Pausig, LMFT, CT

Can you see me? Can you hear me? Can you touch me? The answers to these questions may all be yes or a diverse NO due to the widespread reaches of the COVID-19 pandemic. The reason is we are collectively grieving and mourning as never before known in our current lifetime. First, we must define grief and mourning during a disaster.

Grief is the constellation of internal thoughts and feelings we experience after a significant loss. Grief is what we feel on the inside. Mourning is the outward expression of our grief. This includes the expression of any traumatic thoughts and feelings we might have. (Alan Wolfelt, 2014)

On March 13, 2020, President Trump declared: All 50 states, the District of Columbia, and 4 territories have been approved for major disaster declarations to assist with additional needs identified under the nationwide emergency declaration for COVID-19. Additionally, 32 tribes are working directly with FEMA under the emergency declaration. (FEMA.GOV, 2020)

GRIEF AMPLIFIED

The sight, sound and touch of grief has changed. Our sadness and sorrow, our anger fear and guilt are all normal emotions of grief. The sadness and sorrow we so often experience in uncomplicated grief is becoming a type of chronic sorrow intensified by the direct and indirect compounded losses. Many are experiencing "grief overload", a series of losses in a short amount of time. Anger is normal during these times of heightened emotions. It is easier to be angry than sad and afraid. Guilt is common under anger.

The COVID-19 pandemic has us collectively experiencing an immense range of losses. To name a few: Loss of Health; Loss of Life; Loss of Job; Loss of Food Sources; Loss of Income; Loss of Assets; Loss of Security; Loss of Sense of Safety; Loss of Trust; Loss of Control; Loss of Spontaneity; Loss of Freedom; Loss of Choice; Loss of Predictability; Loss of a Lifestyle, Loss of Rites of Passage (school, proms, graduations) Loss of our Assumptive World; etc.

Perhaps we are grieving the "death" of many of the aforementioned. Merriam-webster.com illustrates one definition of death as the passing or destruction of something inanimate, another is extinction. We are seeing the passing and perhaps extinction of a lifestyle we once knew.

Can you see me in life?
During the quarantine, you can see the people you live with or not if they had to "self-quarantine" from possible exposure. If available, you can communicate over a smartphone video app to "see" your loved ones and friends. The explosion of ZOOMing helped us gather in ways like never before. If you know someone affected by COVID-19 and are or were in the hospital, NO, you

could not see them. Loved ones were separated for many weeks during hospitalization. Loved ones in nursing homes and assisted living facilities were unable to see their loved ones and quarantined in their rooms. One local family accessed a landscapers bucket truck to raise them to a nursing home's third floor window in order to "see" their elderly loved one as they held an "I Love You" sign only a week before that loved one died from COVID-19. People over the age of 60 are now an endangered species as well as those with health issues. We must stay away to lessen the risk of exposure. But it is not the same as seeing our loved ones and friends up close and personal.

MOURNING INTERRUPTED

Can you see me after death?
This too was a NO as memorial services and church services were prohibited and families had to forgo traditional death rituals. Early on families could not gather for a goodbye inside the funeral home. Families gathered in their respective cars, rode to the cemetery, and viewed the burial from their cars. There were no graveside gatherings. No one truly "saw" anyone. If they did, it was behind a newly homemade facemask. Even now with limited gatherings, facemasks, and social distancing prevail the ability to mourn as we once knew. This has become an interruption of a necessary intimate gathering of mourning souls.

Can you hear me?
We hear the wailing of personal and collective grief in voices. We even hear it muffled through the sea of facemasks. We experience the grief of not being able to tell a dying loved one "goodbye".

Can you touch me?
The inability to touch a loved one, hold hands or hug has been a huge loss during this time of quarantine and social distancing. The

sick and dying are tended to by the loving and compassionate medical personnel clad in layers of PPE. Absent is the presence and skin to skin hand holding, face stroking, gentle kissing, and hugging. That kind of touch that says, "I am here", "I love you", "You are going to be okay", "We are going to be okay" and perhaps, "goodbye".

These integral pieces of human connection have been lost between loved ones, friends, neighbors, the community and even friendly strangers during illness, quarantine, self-distancing, and hospitalization.

Alan Wolfelt, PH.D.'s Companioning philosophy helps us be present with the mourner and walk alongside them in this wilderness called grief. In time we will reconcile to this new way by learning to live with our grief and being forever changed.

MOURNING COVID-19 Style
How do we mourn as a family, as neighbors, as a community, as a nation and worldwide without the rituals that have been in place for as long as we know? How do we mourn when we cannot be together?

We mourn with Love. We mourn "together" by any means possible. We are resilient people who have resources within us given by our creator and we have external resources. How do we mourn? We mourn COVID-19 Style, anyway we can think of: Caravan, distanced at the curbside, Zoom, etc. And as we slowly gather once again, in person, together again.

References:
Alan Wolfelt, P. (2014). *Healing your grief when disaster strikes.* Companion Press.
FEMA.GOV. (2020, March 13). *COVID-19 Disaster Declarations, March 13, 2020.* Retrieved from https://www.fema.gov/coronavirus/disaster-declarations

Debbie Pausig, LMFT, CT, is a Licensed Marriage and Family Therapist, a Certified Thanatologist, Professional Support Group Leader for HDSA CT-Chapter and Hospice Bereavement Coordinator for VNA Community Healthcare & Hospice. She is a National Speaker and Author of "An AffaiЯ Worth Remembering With Huntington's Disease, Incurable Love & Intimacy During an Incurable Illness." In 2019 she was quoted in grief articles in the Washington Post and on CBS Radio Network. She is a contributing author in Natural Awakenings Magazine.In 2013, she published a reflective article, "Grieving Behind the Badge, We are the First Responders" for ADEC's publication, The Forum. A reflection on the Sandy Hook Tragedy. Debbie uses humor and compassion drawn from 25 years of experience in Law Enforcement and 17 years as a family caregiver into her profession as a therapist and presenter. www.debbiepausig.mft.com

APPENDIX V:

Will I always feel this bad during the Holiday Season?
There is Hope with these 23 tips
By Debbie Pausig, LMFT, FT updated 11-1-23

It is easy to understand why grief during the holiday season and special occasions is so hard. You are grieving a relationship that has died and the loss of a shared holiday with a special person. How you celebrate is forever changed.

The sights and sounds of the coming holidays are a constant reminder of your life changed. At times, "griefbursts", a power surge of grief, may come out of nowhere. You may feel a disconnection from people, places and the happenings of the season. Even in the midst of a crowd you may feel more isolated & lonelier, as if floating alone on your own island of grief. You may reflect longingly to the past yearning for the return to the way it was, not in the reality of what is. Your world and its traditions, holidays and life are changed forever. What can you do in this world that's called a "new normal"?

Here is a list of 23 practical tips to help make the holiday season a little easier on you and perhaps more meaningful. These are just some ideas to guide you at this difficult time of the year. In time, you may add or remove items or perhaps develop your own list of things that have worked for you. This list is a compilation of my personal grief experiences and professional resources.

Talk About Your Loved One: Get rid of that **GIANT PINK ELEPHANT** in the room. So many people are afraid to speak their loved one's name for fear of upsetting someone. Ask friends and family to share memories of your loved one in photos, stories and mementos. Talking about them honors the relationship and the love that was shared. Talking about them means that they are not forgotten.

K.I.S.S. (Keep It Small & Simple): Find easier ways of tending to others by reducing your expectations. Limit or postpone decorating, baking & dinner preparations.

Shopping: If you must shop, avoid the crowded times. Ask a friend to accompany you for support and distraction. Shop from a catalog or online. Purchase gift certificates. Stop & Shop, Shop Rite, Instacart, Doordash and other food delivery programs have become a great convenience. They are a time & energy saver for many.

Sending Cards & Letters: Shorten your list or omit the task this year.

Accepting Invitations: Be kind to yourself and ease the demands and expectations of the party season. You may not want to accept, attend or participate in all activities. Try to push yourself to attend or participate in a few. Let family members know your plans. Go with a plan such as arriving late & leave early. Drive yourself. Have an "exit plan" if you become overwhelmed. Hosting your own gathering allows you to stay in "your" territory and "you" are in control of the social event.

Traditions: Old & New: Traditions are one of the most difficult things to face during the holiday season. Try exchanging the "old" for something "new". Making changes can make things less painful. Let the children decorate; Change the menu; Change who hosts; Eat out; Attend religious services at a different time, or different church or synagogue; Open gifts at a different location or time; Going away on a short trip may be a welcome & refreshing change of environment.

Be patient: Be kind and gentle with yourself. "Let Go" of the "ought's" & "shoulds", the "anticipations" & "expectations", the "guilts" & "resentments", of the season. Learn to compromise. You just may feel lighter.

Be realistic: Seeing the "empty chair" at the table will hurt. Be ready for the tough moments. Allow yourself to feel them. "Let Go" of the tears and let them flow. You will probably feel better. Decorate your surroundings with boxes of tissues for the tears.

Plan, Plan, Plan Ahead: Grief makes the ability to concentrate more difficult. Make a "list" and prioritize what is important to you!

Listen, To Yourself: Be aware of your needs and ask for help from friends and family. Know who are your "listeners" when you need to talk and "doers" when you need something to get done. You are grieving and it's okay to need and receive caring from others.

Take Care of Yourself: Take part in regular exercise or be a spectator! Eat right; Drink water; Get plenty of rest, grieving is exhausting! Take a nap; Listen to soothing music; meditate; read a light book; take a walk; stare into the night sky; color in a coloring book; paint, spend time with a pet, etc.

Give Yourself Joy: Treat yourself to things that you enjoy. Be responsible in the creation of your own joy. Look at things through a childlike lens where wonder is found everywhere!

Humor: Find something to laugh about. Share a story of one of your grief related fumbles. Ask me about mine!

Create Memories Gifts: Your loved one left "gifts" of memories such as photos, sayings, recipes, stories, companionship, laughter, love, etc. Put these "gifts" in a special box.

Do Something Your Loved One Did: Honor your loved one by doing something special they did. It may take years to master their recipe, storytelling, etc. It creates a new set of memories of you trying.

How to respond to "Happy Holidays": You may choose to say, "I'll try or Best Wishes to you".

Plans CAN Change: Nothing you do this year is etched in stone. Next year may be the same or different. Whatever works for you is okay. Whatever makes you comfortable is okay.

Share Yourself and Your Love with Others: Volunteering or helping the needs of others can be very healing. Bring a meal to a homebound person or elderly neighbor. Collect toys or food for those in need. Helping others helps ourselves.

Pay Attention to Your Inner Clock: Time will lessen pain not your connection with your loved one. Others may want you to "move on" because they are uncomfortable seeing you in pain. It takes time to move through grief. There are no shortcuts or detours around it to avoid it. Take this time to look inward, reflect, and evaluate your meaning and purpose in life.

Light a Special Candle: Light a candle during the holiday season. This special lighting honors the love and life you shared. Remind yourself that you carry the light of that love within you always.

Pain & Fear Management: We feel the pain of our lost loved ones. Doing what is best for you, is the best way to manage the painful symptoms of grief. What is best is different for everyone. Remember this sentence, "I can control what is most comfortable for me". The anxiety of holiday anticipation is usually worse than the "day" itself. A goal is to *"Lose the Pain"*, not the *"Memory of the Person"*.

LOVE, Medicine for "Dis-ease" & "Dis-comfort": I sometimes describe grief as a "Dis-ease" of the heart. This "Dis-ease" disrupts the natural state of ease and balance that my loved one provided. Grief may also cause fear or "Dis-comfort", the absence of comfort. Remembering our loved one, receiving love and comfort from others can help remove the "Dis" allowing ease and comfort back into our hearts and lives. Embrace the love from others who care. You are not alone.

Something to Ponder: Many others may be carrying the weight of grief as well. They hide their sadness behind forced smiles, especially during the Holiday Season. Understand that we <u>can</u> & <u>will</u> get through <u>these</u> days, one moment at a time and one day at a time. We too, like a child, must learn to crawl before we stand and toddle before we walk, again. And, we will fall, and we will get up, again. Our Hope is to run and maybe even skip...... again. And keep moving <u>through</u> this thing called grief.

Please share this tip list with others grieving during this and any holiday season. Sharing knowledge and tips are gifts of love from one to another. Through sharing we help in our own healing, and we learn that we are not alone on this journey.
(Original 2016, updated 11/1/23) Debbiepausigmft.com

Peace,
Debbie

APPENDIX VI:

Surviving to Thriving with Six Essentials
Debbie Pausig, LMFT, CT

When we embark on a journey, we pack the essentials. These are the "go-to" items in what would go into our "carry on" luggage. We have been carrying a lot of luggage the last 2 years during COVID-19. These six must pack essentials will help you care for yourself as we continue to "Survive and Thrive" as we move into the future. Today, we trade that heavy baggage in for something lighter. We will trade in the BIG heavy luggage for a "backpack" or stylish "tote" that will hold six essentials that we need to re-engage and enjoy the outside world once again.

The Six Must Pack Essentials Are:
1. Patience
The journey of the last 2 years has been a long one. No one has ever encountered a time like this. We need a lot of patience as we learn to acclimate being with people once again. The thought of being in close proximity and perhaps unmasked. Do we remember what the beautiful faces of our loved ones, friends and family look like? Most of all, we need patience with ourselves while navigating the changes. Will it be "just like riding a bike?" Our lives have forever been changed. Find your own comfortable pace in this marathon.
2. Humility
"I cannot do this alone". A humble person knows, is aware of, and realizes their limitations. It takes courage and great inner strength to break the silent suffering of going it alone. A humble person knows it is okay to ask for help. All you have to do is ask. Open the door because someone to help will be on the other side to greet you. With a little help, your "backpack" or stylish "tote" will be

lighter to carry on this journey. We are all here to help each other. We are a Team, we are a village.

3. Food, Tea, Blanket & ..

For this new journey, we need sustenance for our own mind, body, and soul. Self-care is the key. We need a healthy diet and know when to rest our mind and bodies. We may brew a cup of favorite tea, have a healthy snack, wrap up in a warm blanket, lose ourselves in a good book and just "be". Taking a Personal Time Out (PTO) to recharge our batteries on a regular basis helps keep us strong to continue this journey.

4. A Doodle Pad

Using a doodle pad, a journal, electronic pad, Budha board or any type of media, jot down or draw your feelings without judging them. Use any creative constructive outlet to let them out. We are human and have feelings that we cannot control. We can control the way we express them in a healthy and safe way. Give your feelings constructive expression and let them flow. It is a great release.

5. Forgiveness

We need to find any extra weight in our "Luggage" that is slowing us down and "LET GO" of it. It is that stuff that will not help us on this journey. Bitterness and resentment are two "weights" we sometimes carry as human beings. Forgiveness lightens our heart. Accepting the reality of life and living one day at a time allows us to focus on what we can do and regain some sense of control again. Forgiveness allows us to "carry on" in the present being available for every precious moment. Now feel that "backpack" or stylish "tote", it IS getting lighter, isn't it?

6. Humor

We need to laugh on this journey at ourselves, with our loved ones, and with those around us. Laughter is a great release. Humor helps us survive. I remember a time I put the toaster in the refrigerator. It was no wonder I could not find it in the pantry! It was clearly time for a break. Yes, I laughed at myself. Can you remember a laughable moment? I recently read that a "6 year old" laughs 300 times a day and adults only 15-100. Let's be 6 again! Pick up some bubbles and have some fun.

Please make copies of these "Six Must Pack Essentials" list and share it with anyone you know who could benefit from these tips.

Sharing knowledge and tips are gifts of love from one human being to another. Through sharing, we learn that we are truly not alone.

In peace and comfort,
Debbie
Debbie Pausig, LMFT, CT (updated Oct. 2023)
Adapted from: Packing for the Grief Journey: Six Essential Items by my colleague, Cheryl Amari, MA.CT., 2014 GriefTeach.com. And, Six Essential series, 2015-present   Debbiepausigmft.com

About the Author

Debbie Pausig, LMFT, CT, Fellow in Thanatology, is a Licensed Marriage and Family Therapist, Hospice Bereavement Coordinator, and NHPCO Bereavement Professional Steering Committee Member.

She has been a keynote speaker and presenter for numerous organizations in CT, RI, NJ and TX.

She was a national speaker, professional support group leader and chapter trainer for the Huntington's Disease Society of America.

She is the author of "An AffaiЯ Worth Remembering With Huntington's Disease, *Incurable Love & Intimacy During an Incurable Illness*." 2014 Edition and the newly released 10th Anniversary Edition.

She has featured contributions in Cancer Today Magazine, Connecticut Women's Consortium-Trauma Matters, Natural Awakenings Magazine, ADEC's the Forum, and the Washington Post.

In 2008, Debbie was trained by the late Sr. Mauryeen O'Brien, O.P, to facilitate the New Day Program for the bereaved which she presented for 7 years at St. Frances Cabrini Church in North Haven, CT Under Sr. Mauryeen's tutelage, she trained future facilitators and conducted workshops on grief in Connecticut.

Debbie uses humor and compassion drawn from 25 years of experience in Law Enforcement, 17 years as a family caregiver and 16 years as a widow into her profession as a therapist and presenter.
Debbiepausigmft.com,
2021 Photo by www.Kelleynorcia.com

ALSO, BY DEBBIE PAUSIG

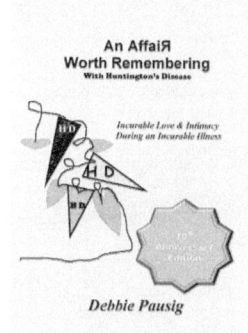

An Affaiꓤ Worth Remembering
With Huntington's Disease
Incurable Love & Intimacy During
 an Incurable Illness
10th Anniversary Edition

This book is Debbie's journey as wife, mother, breadwinner, caregiver and widow/spouse survivor of Huntington's Disease. It is about creating "Awareness" and giving the families affected by Huntington's Disease a "Voice" to a situation that few understand, including friends, family, co-workers, and the community. Huntington's Disease is REAL and knowledge of the disease and its ripple effect on a family is REAL.

Huntington's Disease is a progressive, life stripping hereditary disease for which there is no cure. LOVE is the most powerful medicine available in living with and caring for a person at-risk and in the throes of it. This is a Love Story that illustrates how a marriage and a family can live, survive and thrive with an illness. Humor, frustration and sadness are just a few emotions experienced by the reader. True Love prevails as this disease bruises and batters a family's spirit. Many gifts are discovered during times of illness. Incurable love and intimacy are two such gifts.

This Anniversary Edition has been updated to reflect her 16th year of grief after her husband's death.
Original printing 2014

Paperback ISBN 979-8-9912212-1-4
Ebook ISBN979-8-9912212-3-8

Debbiepausigmft.com

www.ingramcontent.com/pod-product-compliance
Lightning Source LLC
Chambersburg PA
CBHW020248130626
46549CB00005B/2117